RED STAR OVER THE THIRD WORLD

Vijay Prashad

First published in India in 2017 by LeftWord Books, New Delhi

This edition first published 2019 by Pluto Press
345 Archway Road, London N6 5AA

www.plutobooks.com

British Library Cataloguing in Publication Data
A catalogue record for this book is available from the British Library

ISBN   978 0 7453 3966 5   Paperback
ISBN   978 1 7868 0480 8   PDF eBook
ISBN   978 1 7868 0482 2   Kindle eBook
ISBN   978 1 7868 0481 5   EPUB eBook

This book is printed on paper suitable for recycling and made from fully managed and sustained forest sources. Logging, pulping and manufacturing processes are expected to conform to the environmental standards of the country of origin.

Sources for images, as well as references for any part of this book are available upon request. All efforts have been made to ensure that the images used are either out of copyright, or the requisite permissions obtained. Any lapse, if brought to the notice of the Publisher, will be rectified.

Simultaneously printed in the United Kingdom and United States of America

This book is for
BRINDA KARAT
who has guided me
since forever
and continues to
guide me yet.

Contents

Nguyễn Ái Quốc, later Hồ Chí Minh, at the founding conference of the Communist Party of France in Tours (December 1920).

Preface

Tensions ran from one end of the Tsarist Empire to another at the start of 1917. Soldiers at the front, fighting a war that seemed to go nowhere, were in the mood to turn their guns against their rulers. Workers and peasants, struggling to make ends meet, had their hammers and sickles ready to crash down on the heads of their bosses and landlords. The various socialist groups and their clandestine organizations struggled to build momentum amongst the people against an increasingly disoriented and brutal Tsarist regime.

On March 8, 1917, Petrograd faced a shortage of fuel. Bakeries could not run. Working women, in the queues for bread, had to go to their homes and factories empty-handed. The textile women – angered by the conditions – went on strike. It was International Working Women's Day. 'Bread for our children' was one chant. Another was 'The return of our husbands from the trenches'. Men and women from the factories joined them. They flooded Petrograd's streets. The Tsarist state was paralyzed by their anger. These working women began the February Revolution of 1917, which culminated in the October Revolution of 1917 and with the formation of the Union of Soviet Socialist Republics (USSR).

A hundred years have passed since the October Revolution. The USSR, which it inaugurated, only lasted for little more than seventy years. It has been a quarter-century since the demise of the USSR. And yet, the marks of the October Revolution remain

– not just in territories of the USSR but more so in what used to be known as the Third World. From Cuba to Vietnam, from China to South Africa, the October Revolution remains as an inspiration. After all, that Revolution proved that the working class and the peasantry could not only overthrow an autocratic government but that it could form its own government, in its image. It proved decisively that the working class and the peasantry could be allied. It proved as well the necessity of a vanguard party that was open to spontaneous currents of unrest, but which could – in its own way – guide a revolution to completion. These lessons reverberated through Mongolia and into China, from Cuba to Vietnam.

When he was a young émigré in Paris, Hồ Chí Minh, then Nguyễn Ái Quốc, read the Communist International's thesis on national and colonial issues and wept. It was a 'miraculous guide' for the struggle of the people of Indo-China, he felt. 'From the experience of the Russian Revolution,' Hồ Chí Minh wrote, 'we should have people – both the working class and the peasants – at the root of our struggle. We need a strong party, a strong will, with sacrifice and unanimity at our centre'. 'Like the brilliant sun', Hồ Chí Minh wrote, 'the October Revolution shone over all five continents, awakening millions of oppressed and exploited people around the world. There has never existed such a revolution of such significance and scale in the history of humanity'. This is a common attitude in the Third World – sincere emotions that reveal how important this revolution was to the anti-colonial and anti-fascist struggles that broke out in the aftermath of 1917.

In September 1945, when Hồ Chí Minh took the podium to declare freedom for Vietnam, he said simply – 'We are free'. And then, as if an afterthought, 'We will never again be humiliated. Never!' This was the sound of the confidence of ordinary people who make extraordinary history. They refuse to be humiliated. They want their dignity intact. This was the lesson of October.

This is a little book to explain the power of the October Revolution for the Third World. It is not a comprehensive study, but a small book with a large hope – that a new generation will come to see the importance of this revolution for the working class and peasantry in that part of the world that suffered under the heel of colonial domination. There are many stories that are not here and many that are not fully developed. That is to be expected in a book such as this. But these are stories of feeling, mirrors of aspirations. Please read them gently.

The LeftWord Communist History group (Lisa Armstrong, Suchetana Chattopadhyay, Archana Prasad, Sudhanva Deshpande) put this book in gear. Our first volume included essays from the core members as well as from Fredrik Petersson, Margaret Stevens and Lin Chun – all key scholars of the legacy of the October Revolution. Grateful for the guidance and friendship of Aijaz Ahmad, Andrew Hsiao, Brinda Karat, Cosmas Musumali, Githa Hariharan, Irvin Jim, Jodie Evans, Marco Fernandes, Naeem Mohaiemen, P. Sainath, Pilar Troya, Prabir Purkayastha, Prakash Karat, Qalandar Memon, Robin D.G. Kelley, Roy Singham, Sara Greavu, Subhashini Ali, Vashna Jaganath and Zayde Antrim. This book would not have been possible without the theoretical and practical work of my comrades in the Communist Party of India (Marxist). And grateful to Zalia Maya, Rosa Maya, Soni Prashad and Rosy Samuel who made writing most of this book in Kolkata a treat.

The book relies upon a great deal of secondary reading, but also on material from the National Archives of India, the Nehru Memorial Museum and Library, the British Library, the National Archives of the UK, the Russian State Archives for Social and Political History and the Library of Congress. I have also used – extensively – the collected works of Lenin, Marx and Engels, Mao and others. I am grateful to the many scholars who delved into the archival record to produce important work on communists from Chile to Indonesia (thinking of our Communist History group and people such as Amar Farooqui, Ani Mukherji, Barbara Allen, Chirashree Dasgupta, Christina Heatherton, John Riddell, Marianne Kamp, Michelle Patterson, Rakhshanda Jalil, Rex Mortimer, Shoshana Keller, Sinan Antoon, Winston James). The format of this book would be overwhelmed if I had included citations. References for any part of this book are available upon request (vijay@leftword.com). Thanks to Nazeef Mollah for a close reading of the manuscript.

Lenin reading Pravda *in his study at the Kremlin, Moscow (October 16, 1918).*

Eastern Graves

Soviet leaders sat in old Tsarist offices, lush with the architecture of autocracy, but now crowded with the excitement of their socialist ambitions. Lenin would tell Nadezhda Krupskaya that he rarely had a moment of peace. Someone or the other would rush in with a decree to be considered or a crisis to be averted. In June 1920, two Japanese journalists – K. Fussa and M. Nakahira – arrived in Moscow after a long journey across the Asian region of the new Union of Soviet Socialist Republics. They were eager to see Lenin but were not confident that he would have time for them. After a brief wait in Moscow, they were allowed to interview him. Nakahira remembered the interview in his dispatch to the Japanese readers of *Osaka Asahi*. 'I interviewed Mr. Lenin at his office in the Kremlin', he wrote. 'Contrary to my expectation, the decoration of the room is very simple. Mr. Lenin's manner is very simple and kind – as if he were greeting an old friend. In spite of the fact that he holds the highest position, there is not the slightest trace of condescension in his manner.'

Lenin was interested in Japan, asking Nakahira a series of pointed questions about Japanese history and society: 'Is there a powerful landowning class in Japan? Does the Japanese farmer own land freely? Do the Japanese people live on food produced in their own country, or do they import much food from foreign countries?' Lenin asked Nakahira if Japanese parents beat their children as he had read in a book. 'Tell me whether it is true or not. It is a very interesting subject', he said. Nakahira told him that there might be exceptions, but on the whole 'parents do not beat their children in Japan'. 'On hearing my answer', Nakahira wrote on June 6, 1920, 'he expressed satisfaction and said that the policy of the Soviet Government is to abolish this condition'. The Soviets had banned corporal punishment in 1917. On October 31, 1924, the USSR's penal legislation would further lay down that punishment of children, in particular, should not be for the purpose of 'the infliction of physical suffering, humiliation or indignity'.

Other foreign journalists found Lenin to be erudite and honest. He seemed to have nothing to hide. There were problems in the new USSR – the white armies of the imperialist countries had rattled its frontiers, while the older problems of starvation and indignity could not be easily overcome. Impatience with the new regime was in the air. It was to be expected. But high expectations can also produce grave disappointment. This is what Lenin had told the American, the British and the French journalists who had previously come to see him. W.T. Goode of the *Manchester Guardian* found Lenin to have a 'pleasant expression in talking, and indeed his manner can be described as distinctly prepossessing'. The entire office where Lenin worked, Goode wrote, had 'an atmosphere of hard work about everything'.

To the Germans, he bemoaned the failure of the German uprising in 1918-19 to create a social revolution. In October, a million German workers went out on strike and formed *Räte* (Councils), the German equivalent of the Soviets. Sailors of the main German naval fleet in Wilhelmshaven refused to weigh anchor. Their mutiny threatened the German imperial monarchy to the core. Their slogan – again an echo from the Soviets – was *Frieden und Brot* (Peace and Bread). The unfolding of this revolution led to the abdication of the petty German monarchs and, eventually, the emperor. The social democrats proclaimed a republic but halted the revolution by guile and violence. The formation of the Communist Party of Germany in late 1918 came as a result of the revolutionary tempo and the betrayal of the social democrats. A mass demonstration on January 5, 1919, brought hundreds of thousands of people to Berlin, where they wanted to proclaim a revolutionary government. The soldiers in Germany, unlike in Russia, did not walk over to the masses. They remained loyal to the social democratic government of Friedrich Ebert. The two leaders of the Communist Party – Rosa Luxemburg and Karl Liebknecht – were killed ten days later. The revolution failed.

In a letter to the workers of Europe and America published in *Pravda* in January 1919, Lenin wrote that the USSR is a 'besieged fortress so long as the armies of the world socialist revolution do not come to our aid'. Lenin's prose is strong here, as he condemns the 'brutal and dastardly murder of Karl Liebknecht and Rosa Luxemburg' by the social democrats. 'Those butchers', he writes, had gone to the side of the enemy. Germany could have had a revolution if the social democrats had not been congenital betrayers of the cause of the people. If only another European country had broken its capitalist chains, Lenin mused to Nakahira and Fussa, the USSR would not be so isolated.

Inevitably, Fussa asked Lenin, 'Where does communism have more chance of success – in the West or in the East?' Lenin had given this question a great deal of thought, at least since the 1911 Chinese, Iranian and Mexican revolutions. These had overthrown forms of autocracy to produce the fragile republics of Sun Yat-Sen, the Iranian Majlis and Porfirio Díaz. These uprisings had inspired Lenin to write an article in 1913 with the provocative title, 'Backward Europe and Advanced Asia'. No such energy for rebellion seemed available in the United States or Great Britain (except in Ireland during the 1916 Easter Rising), in France or Germany. 'So far', Lenin told Nakahira, echoing the old certainties of European Marxism, 'real communism can succeed only in the West'. But, given the 1911 uprisings from Mexico to China, his own 1916 studies of imperialism and of the use of colonial armies in the Great War of 1914-18, he added, 'it must be remembered that the West lives at the expense of the East; the imperialist powers of Europe grow rich chiefly at the expense of the eastern colonies, but at the same time they are arming their colonies and teaching them to fight, and by so doing the West is digging its own grave in the East.'

Bolsheviks in Petrograd (1917). Support for the Bolsheviks increased exponentially in the months between March and November.

Red October

The Russian Revolution tore through the fabric of time. What should never have been became real – a workers' state, a country whose dynamic was to be controlled by the working class and peasantry. It was not enough to overthrow the Tsar and to inaugurate the rule of the bourgeoisie. Too much sacrifice of the people had gone into the uprisings that produced the February 1917 uprising against the Tsar's rule. A bourgeois revolution was insufficient. It would suffocate the great dreams of the workers and peasants that had been made clear in their slogans. Would the bourgeoisie be willing to end the war and to turn over the land to the people? Would a bourgeois state be willing to put the desperate needs of the people at the forefront of its agenda? It was unlikely. That is why a second revolution took place in October-November of that year. The Soviets seized power. They proclaimed to the world's wretched that this was possible: a country could be ruled by its working people.

Even more remarkable, the new Soviet Union declared that it was not merely formed to uphold the national interests of the people of the Union of Soviet Socialist Republics. 'We claim that the interests of socialism, the interests of world socialism, rank higher than national interests, higher than the interests of the state', said Lenin to the Communist Party's Central Committee in May 1918.

It was this attitude that moved the Russian communists to create the Communist International (1919-43). This International – the Comintern – had as its charge to assist and guide revolutionary forces across the world, to connect them to each other and to amplify their grievances and demands. The October Revolution was certainly authored by the populations ruled over by the Tsar, but its promise was global.

Human history gives us few examples of toilers taking hold of government. Kings and queens saw it as their divine right to rule. The French Revolution of 1789 set aside this expectation. Ordinary people – the mob – pushed themselves out of hunger and war to demand the right to rule. 'Liberty, Equality, Fraternity' was their battle cry. Like the Russian Revolution of 1917, the French Revolution's siren was heard far and wide. In the island of Hispaniola, Toussaint L'Ouverture – born into slavery – led a rebellion of slaves against the French planters. It was the first successful slave rebellion to form a state. There is a direct line that links these late 18th-century rebellions – in France and in Haiti – to the Russian Revolution of 1917. These are its precursors. These rebellions broke the spell of divinity that surrounded the rulers. Ordinary people could rule. That was the lesson of the French and the Haitian Revolutions.

But these revolts of the 18th century took place against early forms of capitalism – when property was being shaped into capital and when merchants dominated over nascent forms of industry. Through the decades after these revolts, the advantages of colonialism, slavery and trade came to the industrialists and some of the old aristocrats. These people used the profits of trade and colonialism to reshape production of goods and services. Harnessing the best of science and technology and taking advantage of workers displaced from farming, the industrialists shaped factory-based production to accumulate more wealth and power. The industrialists and the merchants – the bourgeoisie, in sum – took control not only over the economy but also of politics.

What the ordinary people had done in the French and Haitian Revolution was to overthrow the monarchy, but they were not able to shape history in their image. France's revolution was delivered to the bourgeoisie. Haiti, like Cuba after 1959, faced a vicious embargo from the United States. The United States government worried that a black republic would threaten the essence of the slave order in the United States. That is why on February 28, 1806, US President Thomas Jefferson prohibited all trade with Haiti. It was intended to suppress this republic of free blacks; a hundred and fifty years later, when the US embargoed Cuba, it intended to overpower the first socialist republic – inspired by the October Revolution – in the American hemisphere.

Competitive capitalism produced rapid developments in technology and in production. Vast amounts of goods were created at the same time as the bourgeoisie put immense pressure on workers to earn less and work more. There emerged quite rapidly a problem of overproduction (too many goods produced) and underconsumption (too few goods purchased) – workers toiled to make the plethora of goods but earned far too little to buy them back. One crisis after another tore through the system. Karl Marx's *Capital* (1867) assessed the endemic nature of the crises precisely. Marx saw that capitalism was both devilishly productive and dangerously unstable. It impoverished workers to produce a grand civilization, but through this impoverishment, it undercut its own ability to survive. Solutions to these crises came through the expansion of national militaries and through wars for colonialism and for markets. Famine for the workers was mirrored in the feasts for the bourgeoisie. It was in this context that the heirs of the French and Haitian Revolutions emerged – the workers' movement in the industrial belts and the anti-colonial peasant and worker movement in the colonies. These twin movements would later form the heart of international communism.

It was the Great War of 1914-18 that set the clock faster for international communism. At a small gathering in Zimmerwald,

Switzerland, in 1915, the socialists offered a unique – Marxist – interpretation of World War I. In their Zimmerwald Manifesto, drafted by Lenin, Alexandra Kollontai and Karl Radek, they wrote, 'Irrespective of the truth as to the direct responsibility for the outbreak of the war, one thing is certain: *The war which has produced this chaos is the outcome of imperialism*, of the attempt on the part of the capitalist classes of each nation to foster their greed for profit by exploitation of human labour and of the natural treasures of the entire globe.' This war was not a war of the people, but a war against the people. The Zimmerwald Left urged the working classes to resist the wars, to defy their rulers and create a society in their own image.

The red-hot contradictions of the war provoked a serious crisis in the weakest link of the imperialist chain – in Tsarist Russia. An International Working Women's Day demonstration on March 8, 1917, set off the workers of the main cities into full-scale rebellion. The International Working Women's Day march had been a staple of the world socialist movement over the past decade since the First International Conference of Socialist Women made this call in 1907. In 1917, the Petrograd Inter-district Committee released a pamphlet, calling on women workers to go on strike. It is an impassioned document, whose flavour can be gleaned from these paragraphs,

> Comrades, working women, for whose sake is a war waged? Do we need to kill millions of Austrian and German workers and peasants? German workers did not want to fight either. Our close ones do not go willingly to the front. They are forced to go. The Austrian, English, and German workers go just as unwillingly. Tears accompany them in their countries as in ours. War is waged for the sake of gold, which glitters in the eyes of capitalists, who profit from it. Ministers, mill owners, and bankers hope to fish in troubled waters. They become rich in wartime. After the war, they will not pay military taxes.

Workers and peasants will bear all the sacrifices and pay all the costs.

Dear women comrades, will we keep on tolerating this silently for very long, with occasional outbursts of boiling rage against small-time traders? Indeed, it is not they who are at fault for the people's calamities. They have ruined themselves. The government is guilty. It began this war and cannot end it. It ravages the country. It is its fault that you are starving. The capitalists are guilty. It is waged for their profit. It's well-nigh time to shout to them: Enough! Down with the criminal government and its entire gang of thieves and murderers. Long Live Peace!

The Committee did not expect the vital reaction that they got from the working women. Women workers left their factories in the thousands. Working men and slowly the peasantry came alongside them. Soldiers, who came from these classes, joined in. They decided that this war was not their war. Their real war was against the aristocracy and its authoritarian state. That had to be confronted directly. Two days after International Women's Day, fifty thousand workers in St. Petersburg were on strike. It was the most powerful demonstration of worker power in Russia to date. The Tsarist system collapsed on March 16, just over a week after the International Women's day demonstrations.

Confidence that workers could govern had to be built. Things moved slowly. The first government to take power was headed by an aristocrat – Prince Georgy Yevgenyevich Lvov – and then by a liberal lawyer – Alexander Kerensky. The workers did not go home. The energy of the revolution was quite ferocious. When the Provisional Government seemed to dither on equal rights for women, the Bolshevik leader Alexandra Kollontai wrote in *Pravda*, 'Weren't we women first out on the streets? Why now does the freedom won by the heroic proletariat of both sexes, by the soldiers and soldiers' wives, ignore half the population of liberated Russia?' The League for Women's Equal Rights – led by Poliksena

Shishkina-Iavein – and other political parties held a massive demonstration on March 19 to demand equal rights, which they won only through their resolute struggle. Workers of all political parties – electrified by this energy – formed Soviets or Councils that developed 'dual power', a situation where they created their own institutions that had legitimacy from popular acclamation. Lenin understood that this new situation was the making of the workers. It was their innovation. 'The most highly remarkable feature of our revolution', he wrote in April 1917, 'is that it has brought about a *dual power*. This fact must be grasped foremost: unless it is understood, we cannot advance. We must know how to supplement and amend old formulas, for example, those of Bolshevism, for while they have been found to be correct on the whole, their concrete realization *has turned out to be* different. *Nobody* previously thought, or could have thought, of a dual power.'

What was 'dual power'? The workers could not merely accept the rule of the Provisional Government, then run by Kerensky and the bourgeoisie. Parallel to that Government, in order to satisfy their deeper ambitions, the workers created their own government – the Soviet of Workers' and Soldiers' Deputies. This was a parliament of the working class and the peasantry, not a parliament of the merchants, industrialists and their service class. Lenin saw that this new form – the Soviet – had a direct ancestor in the Paris Commune of 1871. What he did not know is that this form of rule had other ancestors – such as the communes (*quilombo*) created by the insurrection of the slaves in Brazil. These are examples from the history of working people who created their own forms of rule – often democratic – against the hierarchies of the masters of property.

What was of great importance is that the workers found their intellectual in Lenin, who listened carefully to what was going on in the factories and in the streets and drove the Bolsheviks close to the mood of the workers. Lenin had, since the 1890s, been in direct touch with the Bolshevik agitators – the rank and file of his party such as Cecilia Bobrovskaya, Concordia Nikolayevna Gromova-Samoilova and Ivan Babushkin – who showed him the limitations of their work and also what kind of avenues had to be explored to enrich their politics. It was this interaction that fed Lenin with the material for the production of a theory of the Bolsheviks, which armed them for the rapid-moving events from February to October 1917.

Lenin's study of the penetration of capitalism in Russian agriculture (*The Development of Capitalism in Russia*, 1899) showed the class breaks in the peasantry, something not fully grasped by the agrarian populists. He found that 81 per cent of the peasantry were poor, landless peasants whose situation was akin to the industrial proletariat. The existence of this section of the peasantry – the vast mass of the Russian population – suggested that they would be political allies of the industrial proletariat, the working class. Here was the theoretical basis for the worker-peasant alliance. It would form the central political dimension of the Bolshevik party. Lenin would continue to update this information, such as in the long pamphlet from 1908 – *The Agrarian Question in Russia Towards the Close of the Nineteenth Century* – which was not published until 1918 for reasons of censorship.

Lenin's two major political texts – *What Is To Be Done?* (1902) and *One Step Forward, Two Steps Back (The Crisis in Our Party)* (1904) – provided the Bolsheviks with two lessons. First, that it was necessary to create a disciplined party of the working class and agricultural proletariat along with their class allies. Such a party would train its cadre to be amongst the people, build their confidence and prepare for the inevitable spontaneous outbreak of unrest. When people protest, a party's experience and political clarity are necessary to ensure that the movement is not overrun by the apparatus of the state – and by a loss of confidence. Second, that the Social Democratic parties would be ready to swallow the energy of the workers and peasants for their own conciliatory ends. It was necessary to show how the Social Democrats often spoke the language of the people, but they were not grounded in the class instincts and class positions of the workers and the peasants. They would, therefore, betray the workers and peasants cavalierly. A party of the workers and the peasants had to be ready for their spontaneous uprising. When the spontaneous strikes broke out in the St. Petersburg factories in 1896, Lenin argued, the 'revolutionaries *lagged behind* this upsurge, both in their *theories* and in their activity; they failed to establish a constant and continuous organization capable of *leading* the whole movement'. This lag had to be rectified. The party of the Bolsheviks had to be of a 'new type', disciplined, centralized and armed with a strong theory of capitalism, imperialism and socialism. 'Give us an organization of revolutionaries', Lenin wrote boldly and seemingly fantastically, 'and we will overturn Russia'.

The key text that came from Lenin was in 1916, *Imperialism: the Highest Stage of Capitalism*. It was here that Lenin laid out the entanglement of the Tsarist state in the world imperialist system. The tentacles of monopoly capitalism from outside the Tsarist territory had strangled the state. If a workers' government came to power, it would be unable to move an alternative agenda unless it confronted these tentacles of monopoly capitalism, the manifestation of imperialism. The overthrow of the Tsar was essential, of course, but it would be insufficient. A new state, a workers' state, would have to confront imperialism, detach itself from those tentacles and use its own considerable resources for the well-being of its own people. The February Revolution had overthrown the Tsar, but the vacillating government of Kerensky had begun to offer concessions to imperialism. This meant that the Kerensky government was suffocating the essence of the revolutionary process. The choice that lay before the Bolsheviks during the long and confusing summer of 1917 was to either witness the destruction of the revolution or to act to save it from the Russian bourgeoisie, which was unwilling to confront imperialism. In April, Lenin wrote that the point was not the seizure of power by a minority – for that would be merely an unpopular coup. 'We are Marxists,' he wrote, 'we stand for proletarian class struggle against petty-bourgeois intoxication, against chauvinism-defencism, phrase-mongering and dependence on the bourgeoisie.' The goal of the Marxists should be to harness the actual experience of the workers and drive an agenda that would make the worker and peasant power into the power of society. For that, the February revolution had to be saved from minority power – the seizure of power by the bourgeoisie in the service of imperialism.

On April 7, 1917, *Pravda*, the Bolshevik paper, published Lenin's April Theses. These ten points captured the sentiments of the masses who had by strike, mutiny and demonstration brought down the Tsar. It was the theory put forward by the April Theses that drew these masses into the Bolshevik party, which had only 10,000 members in April but half a million members by October.

What were these theses? Here is my summary:

- That the Great War was an imperialist war.
- That the Revolution remained in motion and power would transfer from the bourgeoisie to the workers and peasants.
- That the Provisional Government, the government of capitalists, must not be supported.
- That the Bolsheviks, a minority in the Soviets, had to explain patiently and systematically that the other parties had made errors, and that it was time to transfer 'the entire state power' to the Soviets.
- That the new order could not be grounded in the parliament but a 'republic of Soviets of Workers', Agricultural Labourers' and Peasants' Deputies'. The police, the army and the bureaucracy had to be abolished.

- That all estates must be confiscated and all land nationalized.
- That all banks be amalgamated into a single, Soviet-controlled bank.
- That all social production and the distribution of products should be under the control of the Soviets.
- That the Party hold a Congress and amend its programme.
- That a new International be constituted.

It was clear and precise. Power had to move from the ruling class to the new class that had to rule, the working class and peasantry, the majority of humanity.

By September 1917, there was impatience amongst the working people to seize power. Early that month, as workers and peasants took to their Soviets and passed resolution after resolution for their own government, Lenin wrote, 'insurrection is art'. It was time for an uprising to save the February Revolution. In John Reed's bracing *Ten Days that Shook the World*, he describes the working-class and peasant energy. 'Lectures, debates, speeches – in theatres, circuses, school-houses, barracks. . . . Meetings in the trenches at the Front, in village squares, factories. . . . What a marvellous sight to see Putilovsky Zavod (the Putilov Factory) pour out its forty thousand to listen to Social Democrats, Socialist-Revolutionaries, Anarchists, anybody, whatever they had to say, as long as they talk!' But they also seemed to want something specific – to found a Soviet Republic. It is this specific demand that led to the October Revolution.

The Congress of Soldiers' Representatives wrote to the 2nd All-Russian Congress of Soviets, 'The country needs a firm and democratic authority founded on and responsible to the popular masses. We have had enough of words, rhetoric and parliamentary sleight of hand!' They demanded a second revolution. In October 1917, the working women of Petrograd who had joined the Bolshevik party held a conference. In the room were people like Concordia 'Natasha' Samoilova, Emilya Solnin from the Aivas plant, the spinner Vasina from the Nitka Factory and Vinogradova from the Bassily Island Pipe Factory. These were hard-working women – factory workers and militant revolutionists. They wanted to overthrow the government of Kerensky. They marched to see Lenin in the Smolny, where he lived and worked. 'Take power, Comrade Lenin: that is what we working women want', they said to him. Lenin replied, 'It is not I, but you, the workers who must take power. Return to your factories and tell the workers that.' This is what they did.

In October, the second Russian Revolution broke out – pushed by the Bolsheviks. This was a seizure of power by the Soviets, who dismissed the bourgeois parliament (the Duma) and appointed themselves as the governors of their own society. Lenin went to the Petrograd Soviet to celebrate the seizure of power. What was the significance of this revolution, he asked his comrade workers? 'Its significance is, first of all, that we shall have a Soviet government, our own organ of power, in which the bourgeoisie will have no share whatsoever. The oppressed masses will themselves create a power. The old state apparatus will be shattered to its foundations and a new administrative apparatus set up in the form of the Soviet organizations.'

Here is Lenin putting into a speech before the Soviets what he had argued in his text – *The State and Revolution* – written in August-September 1917, but published the following year. He had read closely Marx's account of the Paris Commune of 1871 as well as the essays by Engels on the state in a socialist society. Engels had suggested that the state must be blown up (*sprengung*), that it could not be inherited in its old form by the proletariat. Old customs of statecraft, embedded in the institutions and practices of the old state, would work like a disease to draw the proletariat into the habits of bourgeois rule. The state had to be 'smashed', 'blown up', somehow transformed into institutions that would conform to the class objectives of the proletariat and the peasants. State institutions were needed in the interim period, but not adopted without transformation. 'The proletariat cannot simply win state power in the sense that the old state apparatus passes into new hands', wrote Lenin in *The State and Revolution*. The revolution 'must smash this apparatus, must break it and replace it by a new one'.

'We've won', sang Mayakovsky in his poem after Lenin's death, 'but our ship's all dents and holes, hull in splinters, engines near end, overhaul overdue for floors, ceilings, walls. Come, hammer and rivet, repair and mend!'

'We destroyed our enemies with weapons, we earn our bread with labour –
Comrades, roll up your sleeves for work' (1920). Poster made by Nikolai Kogout
(1891-1959).

Follow the Path of the Russians!

News travelled slowly to Europe's colonies in 1917-18. India would only get its world news through Britain. Its news services – such as Reuters – came with the worldview of the India House in London. What the British imperialists wanted known would be allowed in the press. The small nationalist press – with readership in the hundreds – tried to articulate an alternative viewpoint, but it suffered from lack of access to information about world events. Gradually, word arrived that the Russian people – mostly peasants – had overthrown the most powerful autocracy in the world, the Tsarist Empire. There was disbelief that men and women with dirt under their fingernails and bodies beaten by machines would be able to come together and seize power. How was this even possible?

Premonitions of 1917 had been available since 1905 when the Russians tried their first major mass revolt against the Tsar. M.K. Gandhi, in South Africa, observed the 1905 uprising with great admiration. The people of Russia, he wrote in *Young India*, are patriotic like the Indians, but unlike the Indians – he felt – they were willing to sacrifice their lives for their dignity. 'The Russian workers and all the other servants declared a general strike and stopped all work', Gandhi wrote. As the workers and servants put down their tools, the Tsar had to make some concessions, for 'it is not within the power of even the Tsar of Russia to force strikers to return at the point of the bayonet. . . . For even the powerful cannot rule without the cooperation of the ruled'. The lesson of non-cooperation came from Russia. It was not the politics of the elite or even merely of urban areas. It was the politics – as far as Gandhi could make out – of the masses, including the peasantry.

1905 ended in failure, although the Tsar did provide some concessions – including the Duma. In India, the contemporary Swadeshi movement – which Gandhi found to be 'much like the Russian movement' – was almost entirely smothered. But even the Swadeshi movement, with its epicentre in Bengal, could not be stopped by British violence as it morphed into deeper and wider struggles against British rule that continued some of its strategies (boycott of British goods, picketing of shops that carried British goods and direct confrontation with British authority). In 1908, the workers in Bombay would go out on strike against their unbearable conditions of work and life. Lenin, on the run from the Tsarist authorities in Finland then Switzerland, observed these strikes and wrote in August of 1908,

> In India, the native slaves of the 'civilized' British capitalists have been recently causing their masters a lot of unpleasantness and disquietude. There is no end to the violence and plunder which is called the British administration of India. Nowhere in the world is there such poverty among the masses and such chronic starvation among the population. The most liberal and radical statesmen in free Britain are, as rulers of India, becoming transformed into real Genghis Khans, who are capable of sanctioning all measures of 'pacifying' the population in their charge, even to *flogging* political dissenters. There is not the slightest doubt that the age-long plunder of India by the English, that the present struggle of these 'advanced' Europeans against Persian and Indian democracy *will harden* millions and tens of millions of proletarians of Asia, will harden them for the same kind of victorious struggle against the oppressors. The class-conscious workers of Europe now have Asiatic comrades whose numbers will grow from day to day and hour to hour.

Europe – in Asia – had, as Lenin wrote in 1913, acted in the most 'backward' fashion – allying with the 'forces of reaction and medievalism' to drive their aims of plunder and profit. Backwardness here implied that it made its alliances with the forces of the past – the landlords and the monarchs – and not the forces of the future – the democratic movement of the masses. It is this European bourgeoisie that was backward, Lenin wrote, because it is committed to 'uphold dying capitalist slavery'. On the other hand – from India to Russia and from China to Persia – Asia is advanced. 'Everywhere in Asia', Lenin wrote, 'a mighty democratic movement is growing, spreading and gaining in strength. The bourgeoisie there is as *yet* siding with the people against reaction. *Hundreds* of millions of people are awakening to life, light and freedom. What delights this world movement is arousing in the hearts of all class-conscious workers, who know the path of collectivism lies through democracy! What sympathy for young Asia imbues all honest democrats!'

Lenin was correct to say that the 'class-conscious' workers in the West supported the struggles from Ireland to India. During the 1913 Dublin Lockout, militant trade unionists in England supported it as part of their own wave of struggles from 1911 to 1914. Twenty thousand workers came to listen to James Larkin speak in Manchester, while English workers raised money for their Irish comrades across the sea. But this did not prevent the bureaucracy of the English workers – in the Trades Union Congress – to refuse to back the strike. 'We asked', wrote James Connolly, 'for the isolation of the capitalists of Dublin and for answer the leaders of the British labour movement proceeded calmly to isolate the working class of Dublin.' This is what Lenin meant when he specifically wrote of the 'class-conscious workers', as opposed to the labour bureaucrats. Suffocated by imperialism, Europe was not fated to be the centre of world revolution. The 'weakest link' had to be found, which Lenin and the Bolsheviks saw in Tsarist Russia. But there was weakness as well in the colonies, where there was hope of revolutionary action to strike a blow against imperialism.

These were the 'Asiatic comrades' needed by the 'class-conscious workers of Europe'.

1917 would succeed. The peasant armies of the Tsarist Empire – including the workers and the soldiers, both a step from the countryside – could not be stopped. If the *muzhiks* could do it, why not the *fellahin*, why not the *campesinos*, why not the *kisans*, why not the *nongmin*?

In Mexico, the revolutionary leader Emiliano Zapata recognized immediately that this Revolution in Russia – a peasant and workers revolution – was related to the Mexican Revolution of 1911 – largely a peasant revolution led by peasant leaders such as himself. 'We would gain a great deal,' he wrote in 1918, 'human justice would gain a great deal, if all people of our America and all the nations in old Europe understood that the cause of the Mexican Revolution, like the cause of unredeemed Russia, is and represents the cause of humanity, the supreme interest of the oppressed.' One of the military chiefs of the Mexican Revolution, in 1919, put the linkage clearly, 'I don't know what Socialism is, but I am a Bolshevik, like all patriotic Mexicans. The Yankees do not like the Bolsheviks; they are our enemies; therefore, the Bolsheviks must be our friends, and we must be their friends. We are all Bolsheviks.' China's Sun Yat-sen would have agreed. 'If the people of China wish to be free', he said on July 25, 1919, 'its only ally and brother in the struggle for national freedom are the Russian workers and peasants of the Red Army.' The Chinese liberal writer Hu Shih wrote in horror, 'Now that the slaves of Confucius and Chu Hsi are declining in number, the slaves of Marx and Kropotkin are taking their place.' Chinese anarchists and revolutionaries of all kinds began to read Marx and Lenin and – after the formation of the Chinese Communist Party in 1921 – began to drift into its orbit.

In December 1917, the Indian journalist K.P. Khadilkar got word of the events in Russia. 'In November, power in Petrograd passed into the hands of those socialists who were led by Lenin and who want a separate peace treaty with Germany', he wrote in *Chitramaya-Jagat*. Khadilkar noted how Lenin's party had secured the support of the soldiers and how Kerensky and his cabinet had been isolated. But then, Khadilkar – a subject of the British Empire – zoomed in on the most important point from this vantage, 'Lenin has issued a decree declaring the rights of nations to self-determination, and freedom has been given to the Baltic states and the Polish people to exercise that right'. In the colonies, the declaration of the right to self-determination was powerful. It defined the revolution.

Subramania Bharati, the revolutionary Tamil poet, sang an ode to 'New Russia',

Life of the people as they themselves order it.
A law to uplift the life of the common man.
Now there are no bonds of slavery.
No slaves exist now.

Some Senegalese soldiers, fighting under the flag of the French empire, decamped for the Soviet Red Army when they heard of its arrival into world history. Boris Kornilov, the Soviet poet, would later sing in his *Moia Afrika* of a Senegalese soldier who died leading the Reds against the Whites near Voronezh 'in order to deal a blow to the African capitalists and the bourgeoisie'. When news of the October Revolution came to the African continent, Ivon Jones of the South African Labour Party and the International Socialist League wrote in *The International*, 'We must educate the people in the principles of the Russian Revolution'. Jones would later be one of the founders of the Communist Party of South Africa. Claude McKay, the Jamaican poet who attended the Fourth Congress of the Comintern in 1922, wrote an essay on 'Soviet Russia and the Negro' in the December 1923 issue of *The Crisis*. Here McKay wrote of what Soviet Russia meant to the liberation of peoples of African descent,

Though Western Europe can be reported as being quite ignorant and apathetic of the Negro in world affairs, there is one great nation with an arm in Europe that is thinking intelligently on the Negro as it does about all international problems. When the Russian workers overturned their infamous government in 1917, one of the first acts of the new Premier, Lenin, was a proclamation greeting all the oppressed peoples throughout the world, exhorting them to organize and unite against the common international oppressor – Private Capitalism. Later on in Moscow, Lenin himself grappled with the question of the American Negroes and spoke on the subject before the Second Congress of the Third International. He consulted with John Reed, the American journalist, and dwelt on the urgent necessity of propaganda and organizational work among the Negroes of the South. The subject was not allowed to drop. When Sen Katayama of Japan, the veteran revolutionist, went from the United States to Russia in 1921 he placed the American Negro problem first upon his full agenda. And ever since he has been working unceasingly and unselfishly to promote the cause of the exploited American Negro among the Soviet councils of Russia.

McKay continued Lenin's agenda at the Comintern's Fourth Congress, where he argued for the necessity of organizing black workers and peasants as well as for the importance of fighting against racism. In his brilliant poem, *If We Must Die*, McKay had written of being surrounded by 'mad and hungry dogs' that seek to brutalize human beings. But this situation of being 'pressed to the wall, dying' is not the conclusion of the story. The ending is simple – 'fighting back!' McKay took inspiration from the October Revolution, from the forthright way that Lenin put forward the demand for all oppressed people to be free and from the fighting spirit of people of African descent in the West to define his optimism.

Without the October Revolution, would the people colonized by Europe have risen up in the way that they did? Would 1919 have been peppered with uprisings of the colonized against

Claude McKay at the Fourth Congress of the Comintern (1922).

their imperial masters – from the uprising in Egypt led by Saad Zaghloul Pasha to the March First Movement in Korea to the May Fourth Movement in China; and then the next year, to the revolt in Iraq against British rule, and then in 1921 the Mongolian Revolution that created three years later the second socialist state in the world? Did they get their confidence from the October Revolution? If not for the class demands from the USSR the Indian National Congress would never have adopted in 1919 the demands of the peasantry. It is certainly true that Gandhi's direct entry into Indian politics with the Champaran Satyagraha (1917) and Kheda Satyagraha (1919) as well as the deep resistance against the Rowlatt Acts and the Jallianwallah Bagh massacre of 1919 steeled the Indian National Congress when it met in Amritsar in December 1919. But at the Congress meeting, the representatives vacillated because the English King had issued a proclamation that appeared sympathetic. The radicals at the Congress – including a young Jawaharlal Nehru – pushed for the peasants who worked the land to be given title to the land and for the peasants to pay tax but no rent. 'Although under the influence of Gandhi we followed another path', wrote Nehru reflectively in his *Soviet Russia* (1927), 'we were influenced by the example of Lenin'.

Ghulam Rabbani Taban, a communist and member of the Progressive Writers Association in India, recalled reading Nehru's *Soviet Russia* (1927) and Rabindranath Tagore's letters from Russia while he was in college. These texts, he said, 'gave a glimpse into a fairy-tale world'. 'During the closing years of the 1920s', he wrote, 'while still at school, we at times heard some fragmentary stories about Russia that trickled through colonial censors. The news of the Russian revolution and its achievements thrilled us. I had no perception of a revolution but the term had been familiarized by the full-throated cries of *Long Live Revolution* ringing throughout the country'. Taban heard Mohammed Iqbal's poems on Lenin, particularly his powerful *Farman-i-Khuda* (God's Command), which starts, '*uttho meri dunya ke gharibon ko jaga do*' – Rise, awaken the poor of my world. And then,

> *Jis khet se dehqaan ko muyassir nahein rozi,*
> *Uss khet ke har khosha-i-gandam ko jalla do.*
> Find the field where the peasants can't get their daily bread,
> And burn every grain of wheat from that field!

Here is the cadence of revolution, the anger at the world as it is, the hope that the fires of revolt will *smash* the state and produce a new order. This is the voice of the small farmer, the landless peasant, the poor of the countryside who are eager to shake the world. And then the poem by Iqbal ends, '*Adaab-i-junoon Shair-i-Mashriq ko sikha do* (Teach the poet of the East the spirit of inspiration!)' – what new languages the artist can learn from the uprising of the poor!

A young Mao, in China, would look longingly to the Russian experience. He would join the movement after the uprising of 1911 that overthrew the Emperor and his rule. Later, after the long war that brought the communists to power in 1949, Mao would reflect on the Russian inspiration. 'Many things in China were the same as, or similar to, those in Russia before the October Revolution. There was the same feudal oppression. There was similar economic and cultural backwardness. Both countries were backward, China even more so. In both countries alike, for the sake of national regeneration progressives braved hard and bitter struggles in their quest for revolutionary truth. . . . The October Revolution helped progressives in China, as throughout the world, to adopt the proletarian world outlook as the instrument for studying a nation's destiny and considering anew their own problems. Follow the path of the Russians – that was their conclusion.'

The cover of Manuel Maples Arce's *Urbe*, designed by Jean Charlot (1922).

The Lungs of Russia

Mexico's Manuel Maples Arce and his fellow *Estridentistas* shrugged off their fellow writers who wanted to emulate European modernism or its classical traditions. They looked elsewhere, deep into the heart of the Mexican revolutionary tradition that opened up in 1911 and outwards toward the Soviet Union. In 1924, Maples Arce wrote a sublime and complex poem – *Urbe: Super-Poema Bolchevique en Cinco Cantos* (*City. Bolshevik Super-Poem in Five Cantos*). Here was language stuttering against the old forms, looking for new terms, new idioms, new ways to express the new world that they wanted to produce.

> *Los pulmones de Rusia*
> *soplan hacia nosotros*
> *el viento de la revolución social.*
> Russia's lungs
> blow the wind
> of social revolution toward us.

The poem – dedicated to the 'workers of Mexico' – echoed the impatient style of Vladimir Mayakovsky, who also felt that the old language – steeped in feudal culture – was not adequate to the revolutionary era. Old Russian was saturated with feudal implications, just as the hierarchies of the system produced bodies that were filled with subservience, the hunched shoulders, the head downcast. But the new Russia had a new attitude. Krupskaya recounted the 'altered language' she heard from women workers and peasants at a meeting. The speakers, she recounted, 'spoke boldly and frankly about everything'. How to speak boldly now as poets, as artists, as actors, as designers? People like Mayakovsky – 'hooligan communists' Lenin called them affectionately – produced novel work, inventive work, work that tried to find itself in the atmosphere of radical democracy.

It is what appealed to people like Maples Arce in Mexico City and the remarkable group in China – Ding Ling, Lu Xun, Hu Yepin and Shen Congwen. During the Russian-Japanese war in 1904-05, Lu Xun saw a picture of Chinese prisoners being led by Japanese troops. 'Physically, they were as strong and healthy as anyone could ask', Lu Xun wrote of the Chinese, 'but their expressions revealed all too clearly that spiritually they were calloused and numb'. It was to break this numbness that he began to write.

It was to break the numbness that Nazrul Islam, the communist poet of Bengal, wrote his triumphant song *Bidrohi* (Rebel) in December 1921. Nazrul Islam, with Muzaffar Ahmad, Abdul Halim and others, went – as Halim put it – on an 'unknown path', frustrated with the present and eager to create the future. These early communists, as the historian Suchetana Chattopadhyay called them, were surrounded with literary magazines with names that evoke that desire for a new opening – *Bijali* (Lightning) and *Dhumketu* (Comet). The police read *Dhumketu* and described it quite accurately, 'the whirlwind energy of the style and inflammatory character of the language had a great unsettling effect on premature and unbalanced minds, with whom the paper was immensely popular'. The journal was edited by the communists, but with Nazrul Islam in the lead. His poem – *Bidrohi* – carries the urgency of Mayakovsky and Maples Arce, of the poets of revolutionary electricity,

> In one hand of mine is the tender flute
> While in the other I hold the war bugle!
> I am the Bedouin, I am the Chengis,
> I salute none but me!

. . .

Maddened with an intense joy I rush onward,
I am insane! I am insane!
Suddenly I have come to know myself,
All the false barriers have crumbled today!

. . .

I am the rebel eternal,
I raise my head beyond this world,
High, ever erect and alone!

This desire to write against the numbness was what would draw in writers from China to Chile, eager to find new language to keep up with the kind of left-wing futurism of the Soviets. It is the sound that one hears from Nazrul Islam, surely, but also from the bursting imagery of the Chilean poet Pablo Neruda, the 'nervous montage' cinema of the Cuban filmmaker Santiago Álvarez or later the dream-like memoirs of the Iraqi communist writer Haifa Zangana.

Maples Arce wrote at a particularly exciting time in Mexico's history. From 1920 to 1924, powerful struggles of peasants and workers forced the Mexican government to deepen its revolutionary commitment. When the government – such as of Álvaro Obregón (1920-24) – vacillated between a revolutionary agenda and a reformist one, the organized working class and peasantry fought them to conduct land reforms and to pursue cultural and educational policies that favoured the masses. With 90 per cent of Mexico illiterate, visual and theatrical arts were necessary to transmit the values of the revolution. It was during the early 1920s that artists began to paint Mexican public spaces and actors began to take their theatre on the road, when educators went to rural areas to teach and when land reform provided the material basis for dignity in the countryside. All of this was to promote the values of the 1911 Mexican Revolution despite the hesitancy of the leadership that emerged. In this time came the murals of Diego Rivera, David Alfaro Siqueiros and José Clemente Orozco, the paintings of Frida Kahlo and the photography of Tina Modotti and Manuel Álvarez Bravo.

Many of these artists were members of the Mexican Communist Party and they were members of the Syndicate of Technical Workers, Painters and Sculptors, whose manifesto said that Mexican art is great because it 'surges from the people, it is collective'. It would break hierarchies, straighten spines, loosen tongues. Maples Arce sensed the importance of this period,

> *La muchedumbre sonora*
> *hoy rebasa las plazas comunales*
> *y los hurras triunfales*
> *del obregonismo*
> *reverberan al sol de las fachadas.*
> Today the resounding crowd
> floods the public squares
> and the triumphant shouts
> of Obregonism
> reflect the sun from the facades.

The crowd in the squares were mainly peasants. It was these peasants who would be the subject of so much revolutionary Mexican art – and of Mexican state policy in these early years.

Twenty years later, in May 1942, Mao gave a series of lectures to the Yenan Forum on Literature and Art. Mao had closely read Lenin's exhortation from 1905 that the new revolutionary literature might serve 'the millions and tens of millions of working people – the flower of the country, its strength and its future'. He was sympathetic to the fact that, like Russia and Mexico, China was a country with high illiteracy. Mao was clear that the revolutionary movement had two armies – the army of guns, which had fought to secure the base area of Yenan, and the army of pens, which would need to provide another kind of armour for the working class and

Frida Kahlo, Marxism Will Give Health to the Sick *(1954).*

the peasantry. Writers and artists have to go to the people, Mao said, in order to understand the people rather than imagine a fantasy population that would remain outside their imagination. 'China's revolutionary writers and artists, writers and artists of promise, must go among the masses; they must for a long period of time unreservedly and wholeheartedly go among the masses of workers, peasants and soldiers, go into the heat of the struggle, go to the source, the broadest and richest source, in order to observe, experience, study and analyze all the different kinds of people, all the classes, all the masses, all the vivid patterns of life and struggle, all the raw materials of literature and art.' It was amongst the people that the artists and writers would learn not only about the social contradictions in the heart of the masses, but they would also learn the imagination of the masses and so produce art for that imagination.

The task of the revolutionary intellectuals is to 'collect the opinions of these mass statesmen' – namely the people – 'sift and refine them, and return them to the masses, who then take them and put them into practice'. This is what the Italian Communist Antonio Gramsci, writing in his prison cell at around this same time, called *elaboration* – to take the views of the masses and elaborate them from common sense to philosophy. Through wall newspapers and pamphlets and through theatre and songs by revolutionary troupes would the intellectuals transfer this popular philosophy back to the masses. 'Writers and artists concentrate such everyday phenomenon,' lectured Mao, 'typify the contradictions and struggles within them and produce works which awaken the masses, fire them with enthusiasm and impel them to unite and struggle to transform their environment.' Mao perhaps had in mind the poetry of Tian Jian, whose *If we didn't fight* (1938) was already a great favourite in Yenan,

If we didn't fight,
The enemy with his bayonet

Would kill us,
And pointing to our bones would say:
'Look,
These were slaves'.

Tian Jian and his comrades pioneered the 'street poetry' festivals, where the poets would gather on the streets to enliven the public space with their poetry. When morale amongst the people was low, Tian Jian, He Qifang, Guo Xiaochuan, Ke Lan, Li Ji and Ai Qing believed, it was the role of the artists to lift the spirit of the masses. There were idioms of the villages in their poems, rhythms familiar to the people but now rendered into more sophisticated rhymes with a clear political purpose. 'A flock of goats follows the goat at the head', sang Li Ji. 'Throughout north Shaanxi, the Communists spread'.

In the crucible of revolutions – whether Russia after 1917 or China in the 1940s or Cuba after 1959 – literature underwent a major transformation, with revolutionary artists tugging at the strings of reality, finding new ways to say new things. Artists and writers tried to fan the flames of revolutionary change and understanding. Their audience was not the old aristocrats or the bourgeoisie, but it was the workers and the peasants who wanted a soundtrack for their revolution, a history and a novel of their actions on the streets.

Russian peasants demonstrate in the Red Square, Moscow (1917).

Peasant Soviets

Lenin understood the limitations of European Marxist orthodoxy. It assumed – from a rigid reading of Marx – that the agent of history was to be the proletariat, seen narrowly as the industrial worker in the trade unions. Concentration on building trade unions was seen, by some socialists, to be sufficient. Lenin called this *economism*. He had a broader vision. The entire working class and the agricultural proletariat needed to be drawn into the struggle through a range of avenues, not just through trade unions. Unions are essential, but they can also narrow the perspective of workers, leading them into battles to increase their wages and improve their working conditions. What was needed was to widen the consciousness of the workers and the agrarian proletariat to see the struggle as one for the totality of humanity. Workers, Lenin wrote, should not seek a better deal within the restricted confines of capitalism, but seek to build a better world within the much broader horizon of communism.

Marx had several times in his writings and speeches indicated that his vision for political change was not rooted only in the trade unions and in trade union struggles. In 1865, Marx gave a speech where he laid out the main themes of his political economy. In that speech, he spoke directly to the trade unions – the crucial bulwark of the class struggle. The unions, he said, 'ought not to forget that they are fighting with effects [and] not with the causes of these effects . . . They ought, therefore, not to be exclusively absorbed in these unavoidable guerrilla fights incessantly springing from the never-ceasing encroachments of capital.' What the unions had to do, Marx said, was to fight on the terrain of politics, to abolish the wage system for a new order. But to get to that point, the strikes and the struggles operated as schools for the working class, a place to develop confidence and learn about the structure that dominated workers and the peasants.

Political change was not to be confined to reforms but expanded to a revolutionary horizon – to *politics*. The immense majority, Marx would frequently write, had to rise up to overthrow the shackles of the present world order. The proletariat – the workers who sold their labour power – would play a crucial role in the socialist revolution. Narrow political democracy was possible under capitalism, where elections could be constrained to advantage the elites. But much broader democracy – including social and economic democracy – was not possible. Such wide democracy would threaten the narrow and selfish control of property by a small minority, who hired labour to enhance their own private property rather than to democratically improve the livelihood and meet the ambitions of the workers. This barrier made the struggles of the proletariat central to the socialist revolution. The bourgeoisie – the owners of capital – would not be willing to widen democracy. They preferred it in chains.

For Lenin, the role of the peasant was crucial. His first major study – *Development of Capitalism in Russia* (1899) – was rooted in the question of the peasantry. Russia was, as they said in those days, a peasant society. Ignoring the role of the small peasantry and the proletarianization of the peasantry would mean missing the revolutionary potential that slumbered in the countryside. In 1905, in an important intervention in *Novaya Zhizn*, Lenin pointed out that the peasants wanted 'land and freedom'. This demand must be met in full, Lenin said, but it had to be extended to a demand for socialism. All peasants do not side with the workers who wage a direct struggle against the rule of capital. It is, he said, the role of the party to draw the small peasants into an active alliance with the workers towards socialism.

It was not hard to see the grief in the countryside. Lenin's friend, Maxim Gorky, pointed out that the peasants called their work *strada* – from the Russian verb *stradat*, to suffer. But to organize suffering was not sufficient. The peasant rising in 1905 showed their capacity. Gorky would write, 'People who think that the peasants are unable to take an active part in the social and political life of the country do not know the peasants'.

In 1920, Lenin looked east and said, 'Soviets are possible there. They will not be workers but peasant Soviets or Soviets of the toilers'. On February 17 of that year, the Indian Revolutionary Association – peopled by émigrés within the USSR such as Raja Mahendra Pratap Singh, Abdul Hafiz Mohammed Barakatullah and Maulana Ubaidullah Sindhi – sent a note to Lenin. 'Indian revolutionaries express their deep gratitude and their admiration of the great struggle carried on by Soviet Russia for the liberation of all oppressed classes and peoples, and especially for the liberation of India', the Association resolved. Lenin wrote a reply to this resolution, which was broadcast on May 10,

> I am glad to hear that the principles of self-determination and the liberation of oppressed nations from exploitation by foreign and native capitalists, proclaimed by the workers' and Peasants' Republic, have met with such a ready response among progressive Indians, who are waging a heroic fight for freedom. The working masses of Russia are following with unflagging attention the awakening of the Indian workers and peasants. The organization and discipline of the working people and their perseverance and solidarity with the working people of the world are an earnest of ultimate success. We welcome the close alliance of Muslim and non-Muslim elements. We sincerely want to see this alliance extended to all the toilers of the East. Only when the Indian, Chinese, Korean, Japanese, Persian and Turkish workers and peasants join hands and march together in the common cause of liberation – only then will decisive victory over the exploiters be ensured. Long live a free Asia!

The question of peasant and worker unity sat in the foreground of this message and in the guidance that came from the USSR to the anti-colonial movements. There could be no motion in their 'peasant societies' if they ignored the vast mass of their population, the peasantry. Those who came from other 'peasant societies', from India and China or from Mexico and Egypt, saw in the Russian Revolution and its first decade of dramatic human development the mirror of their own aspirations.

India's Jawaharlal Nehru, leader of the Congress Party, arrived in the USSR to celebrate its tenth anniversary. He marvelled at the ability of this 'peasant society' to rapidly move from misery to fellowship, from starvation to surfeit. Russia interested Nehru because both India and the USSR were peasant countries with poverty and illiteracy as the barriers to freedom for the people. What he saw in 1927 surprised him, that there was less poverty in the country than he imagined and that the leadership had come from amongst the workers and peasants. Mikhail Kalinin, whom Nehru met, came from a peasant family and was then the head of state of the USSR. Joseph Stalin, the head of government, came from a family of cobblers and housemaids. These were ordinary people, who now ran an extraordinarily large country. Of his visit, Nehru wrote, 'Russia thus interests us, because it may help us to find some solution for the serious problems which the world faces today. It interests us specially because conditions there have not been, and are not even now, very dissimilar to conditions in India. Both are vast agricultural countries with only the beginning of industrialization, and both have to face poverty and illiteracy. If Russia finds a satisfactory solution for these, our work in India would be made easier.'

And indeed, Nehru found that the USSR had made great gains against hunger and poverty and towards increasing the power and dignity of the peasantry. From great poverty and deprivation, the USSR quit the Great War, fought off the invasion of the capitalist powers and struggled to build up the industrial and agricultural

'Woman, learn to read and write! – Oh, Mother! If you were literate, you could help me!' *Likbez Poster (1923) made by Elizaveta Kruglikova. Likbez, abbreviation for 'likvidatsiya bezgramotnosti', meaning 'elimination of illiteracy', was a hugely successful Soviet programme for spreading literacy.*

capacity of the country. Within a decade, the USSR was able to move from extreme backwardness to a situation of economic and social stability. Nehru looked carefully at the statistics on access to medical care, life expectancy, infant mortality and industrial growth. These showed improvement. But these were not conclusive. What interested him, the keen observer, were the signs of a much richer social life for the peasants. 'They have their newspapers and country fairs and academies and sanatoria; their libraries and reading rooms and women's clubs. The Society for the Liquidation of Illiteracy and Mutual Aid Societies are to be found everywhere. And so are the youth organizations – the Pioneers and the Komsomols' – the All-Union Pioneer Organization and the Young Communist League. This richness, this wealth, was the best measure of advance.'

Without literacy, Lenin wrote, 'there can be no politics; without [literacy] there are rumours, gossip, fairy-tales and prejudices'. In 1897 – in the last Tsarist census – less than a third of Russians counted as literate (only 13 per cent of women were literate). In 1917, a third of men were literate and less than a fifth of women. Immense amount of the social surplus in the USSR was turned over to education and health, to the basic needs of the population. By 1926, thanks to the Likbez programmes, half the population could read and write. By 1937, two decades into the Revolution, the literacy levels rose to 86 per cent for men and 65 per cent for women. It was an extraordinary achievement. It needs to be mentioned that the USSR followed the policy of indigenization (*korenizatsiya*) – promoting regional languages so that people could develop their knowledge and wisdom in their native tongues and not merely in Russian. Such advance took place in a 'peasant society'. India's literacy rate at the close of two centuries of British colonial rule stood – in comparison – at 12 per cent.

Khazir minda azad! Now I too am free! (1918-1920)
Courtesy: British Library.

Soviet Asia

The October Revolution certainly began in the cities of St. Petersburg and Moscow. In June 1916, nonetheless, unrest broke out in the Kazakh steppe and Turkestan against the Tsar's attempt to conscript the people of Central Asia into his futile European war. In Ferghana Valley and into the areas of the Kazakh and Kirghiz, the people attacked Russian settlers and then fled – *en masse* – into China's Xinjiang. Chinese secret societies – rooted in anti-monarchical ideas – had infiltrated Central Asia. One such society was the Gelaohui, which had been brought to Xinjiang by the Hunan army of Zuo Zongtang. One of the members of the Gelaohui was Mao's main general, Zhu De. When asked about Bolshevism and its impact on the organization of the Chinese Communist Party, Zhu De told the American communist Agnes Smedley that 'the cell system was as old as the Chinese secret societies'. He would know. He was a Great Elder of the Gelaohui lodge in Sichuan till he became a communist. The Gelaohui and the Red Spears moved between Central Asia and China, inculcating the view that the Tsar must be overthrown. The October Revolution had its origins, then, not only in St. Petersburg but also in Qaraqol (Kazakhstan).

Many Russian settlers in this region, uneasy about the revolts around them, joined the White Army to overthrow the October Revolution. The Soviets sent a Commission to investigate the situation in Turkestan. It recommended that the old Tsarist bureaucrats be removed from the area, that colonialist attitudes amongst the Russian settlers be eliminated and that the old feudal and patriarchal attitudes amongst the Central Asians be combatted. Tensions between Turkestan and Moscow prevailed.

The communists in Tashkent – such as Turar Ryskulov, Mirsaid Sultan-Galiev and later Zeki Velidi Togan – fought for the autonomy of their region from Moscow and for a much less hostile position towards the elites of the Turkmen people. Moscow was not keen on this. Its representatives in the Commission – no Turkmen amongst them – wanted to integrate the area into the USSR and to move towards a much fiercer politics of class struggle. Lenin felt that the local communists had a better sense of the ground than his own comrades in Moscow. In his note to the 'Communists of Turkestan', Lenin wrote,

> The attitude of the Soviet Workers' and Peasants' Republic to the weak and hitherto oppressed nations is of very practical significance for the whole of Asia and for all the colonies of the world, for thousands and millions of people. I earnestly urge you to devote the closest attention to this question, to exert every effort to set an effective example of comradely relations with the peoples of Turkestan, to demonstrate to them by your actions that we are sincere in our desire to wipe out all traces of Great-Russian imperialism and wage an implacable struggle against world imperialism, headed by British imperialism.

The idea of 'Great Russian imperialism' was crucial for the territory of the former Tsarist Empire. Central Asia had to be a model for a post-colonial world. Soviet troops routed the local kings of Khiva and Bukhara, putting in place of the monarchs the Khorezm People's Soviet Republic and the Bukharan People's Soviet Republic (both later incorporated into the Uzbek and Turkmen Soviet Socialist Republics). These republics – based on the policy of self-determination – needed to guard their autonomy carefully.

Uneasiness remained at the heart of the Central Asian areas. Questions of religious freedom and the rights of the small proprietors dogged the Soviet project. The Young Bukharans and the Young Khivans – such as Abdulrauf Fitrat, Fayzulla Khodzhayev and Akmal Ikramov – were impatient to transform the structure and culture of their societies. For them, the Soviet promise meant that their societies – mired in feudalism – could be wrenched into an egalitarian era. The Indian writer L.G. Ardnihcas travelled through Central Asia two decades later and found that 'the early Bolsheviks made many mistakes of policy and procedure. They were imbued with a sense of superiority that was almost fatal to the cause'. At the Congress of the Toilers of the East at Baku in 1920, Grigory Zinoviev came to the heart of the problem in Central Asia. The most important issue, he said, was land reform. Zinoviev felt that the Central Asian peasantry was too timid to take action. 'Centuries of stagnation' as a result of 'many centuries of oppression and slavery on the part of Europeans', he said in his speech to the delegates, had halted the peasantry. 'The solution of the land question in the East', he said, 'is surrounded with considerable difficulties which arise partly because the peasants, beaten and terrified by their oppressors, have not dared to take decisive revolutionary action'. It is here that the Bolsheviks had to act.

In the Azerbaijan Republic, for instance, where the Soviet system is already in force, there are still peasants who fear to seize the land for themselves, being afraid of the revenge of the bourgeoisie and the landlords. The same difficulty is to be met in Turkestan where there are still Russians who were sent by Tsarism and the bourgeoisie especially to oppress the natives. This part of the inhabitants, not wishing to abandon its privileges, continues to act as before, though frequently covering itself with Soviet and Communist watchwords. The problem confronting all true representatives of the Soviet is to denounce these gentry and show the native peoples that Soviet Russia will not tolerate the former colonial policy of robbery, but is the bearer of culture and civilization in the best sense of the words. This we do, not after the fashion of the old colonists, but as elder brothers bringing light and culture.

These 'elder brothers' were not Russian chauvinists, but Central Asians who had turned to Communism. The Soviets trained local men and women at the Communist University of the Toiling East (KUTV) in Moscow. These men and women then returned to their homes and developed – to the extent that they found possible – a Central Asian communism. The Communist Party, Ardnihcas wrote in *The Soviet East*, 'decided to have its hands made of local flesh and blood and to discard the hand thrust from outside into the national republics'.

One of these republics was that of the Kyrgyz people, who lived between the USSR and China. When the Kara-Kyrgyz Autonomous Oblast was created in 1924, the Kyrgyz people had no alphabet for their language (although some used the Arabic script, but only rarely). Within a few years, the new Soviet introduced a Latin-based alphabet. As Raymond Steiger and Andrew Davies noted in 1942 in their book *Soviet Asia*, 'Until a few years ago, there was no written alphabet of the Kirghiz language; the great majority of the people was illiterate. Today, the Kirghiz have an alphabet, and in 1939 there were 20,000 pupils in the republic's 1,500 elementary schools, 119 high schools, and three universities. More than 20,000 teachers gave instruction in the native language from books printed in the new alphabet'. 'It is the common people, the peasant, the labourer and the nomad shepherd,' Ardnihcas wrote, 'who have taken the lead in the achievement of the great transformation'.

Remarkable achievements of massive scale improved the lives of the peoples of Soviet Asia. The 1,500-kilometre Turkestan-Siberia (Turksib) Railway ran from Tashkent (Uzbek Soviet Socialist Republic) to connect with the Trans-Siberian Railway.

This mammoth project went from 1926 to 1931 as part of the First Five-Year Plan of the USSR. A documentary of the construction – made by Viktor Turin and released in 1929 as *Turksib* – is a superb exploration of the problems faced by the nomadic peoples of the region and how the railway would lift some of their burdens. Ghafur Ghulam, later the National Poet of the Uzbek Soviet Socialist Republic, watched the train project come to fruition and wrote an ode to its importance (it was translated in 1933 by the African American communist poet Langston Hughes and his neighbour, the Georgian sculptor Nina Zorokovitz). 'Crushed by the bronze five-pointed heart of the locomotive', he wrote, 'along these ancient roads which have seen so many things' would now come the proletariat of Asia. They will now travel on a 'steel caravan in union and solidarity'.

> These ancient roads are our immortality.
> And along these roads
> Will pass the gale of liberty
> And not the smell of blood.

Turin's documentary and Ghulam's poem celebrate the immense social labour of the Central Asian people who were now creating projects for their own benefit. But this train was not the only major project. The 300-kilometre Great Ferghana Canal (completed in 1939) helped draw water from the Syr Darya River to the cotton fields of the Ferghana Valley in the eastern part of the Uzbek Soviet Socialist Republic. It would allow the expansion of agriculture in that region, drawing in farmers from across Central Asia to the fertile valley.

None of these gigantic projects could have been conceived if the various republics were not linked together into the USSR. In hindsight, there is a great deal of criticism of the environmental problems from the Soviet-era fertilizer industry near the Aral Sea

Red Caravan (1939), photograph by Max Penson (1893-1959).

and of the use of industrial chemicals in the soil in the Ferghana Valley. This is, of course, true, but it not a problem solely of the communist experiment.

Inspiration for the common people of Central Asia came from the Soviet decrees that echoed off the walls of the colonies, their titles illustrative enough:

To All the Muslim Workers in Russia and the East (November 1917).
Declaration of the Rights of the Peoples of Russia (December 1917).
Declaration of the Rights of Workers and Exploited People (January 1918).

The declaration of December 1917 was most powerful. It called not only for 'the equality and sovereignty of the peoples of Russia' but also 'the right of the peoples of Russia to free self-determination, even to the point of separation and the formation of an independent state'. This was unimaginable in the colonies. When US President Woodrow Wilson tried to take credit for the ideas of peace without annexation and for self-determination, the Indian journalist and nationalist K.P. Khandilkar wrote in *Chitramaya-Jagat*, 'Lenin did it more than two years ago'.

By late 1919, even those who had either put their faith in Wilson, or who had used Wilson's words, found themselves disappointed. China's Mao, then a young man, saw the European leaders as 'a bunch of robbers' who 'cynically championed self-determination'. Lenin's USSR, in this period, did not have the same kind of institutional limitations as Wilson's USA. Wilson's test came at the League of Nations meeting in Paris, where he helped squelch the Japanese bid to have a Racial Equality Clause at the heart of the League of Nations Covenant. Wilson's emissaries proceeded to bury that Clause, damaging the League of Nations and putting aside the universalism of his own proposals for self-determination. Racism was vital to the capitalist policies of the United States and the European countries that relied upon ideas of racial superiority to maintain their colonies and semi-colonies as places of super-exploitation of people and nature. No question of giving these places freedom. Wilson sent in the United States military to occupy Nicaragua in 1914, Haiti in 1915 and the Dominican Republic in 1916. In 1913-14, Wilson intervened militarily in Mexico to undermine its revolution. The unseemliness of Wilson's imperialist military actions irked Wilson's Secretary of State Robert Lansing, who wrote to his president in 1916, 'It seems to me that we should avoid the use of the word *Intervention* and deny that any invasion of Mexico is for the sake of intervention.' Wilson's advisor, George Louis Beer, encouraged him not to allow his own rhetoric to imply self-determination for African states. 'The negro race', wrote Beer, 'has hitherto shown no capacity for progressive development except under the tutelage of other peoples.' In this list of other peoples were the British and French – who had experience – as well as the Scandinavians – who had a clean reputation. The people of Africa and Asia, however, were 'not yet able to stand by themselves under the strenuous conditions of the modern world'. Wilson was the contemporary of the Bolsheviks. Their world was alien to his.

The Communist International met for the first time in March 1919; it snubbed Versailles and Wilson. They were not relevant to it. It charted a different course that culminated at the Baku Conference of the Toilers of the East (1920). The Bolshevik Mission in Tbilisi (Georgia) offered the following description of the conference,

> The first sitting of the Conference was devoted to Zinoviev's speech, which explained the aims of the Conference. The passage in Zinoviev's speech where he invited the Eastern peoples to a holy war was interrupted by the demonstrations of the delegates who in an ecstasy jumped from their seats, unsheathed their swords and waved them in the air. The hall was filled with cheering in all languages. For many minutes, to the strains of the *Internationale*, the Conference

swore to keep faithful to the cause of the working classes. The sitting was very enthusiastic, and was frequently interrupted by ovations.

In the evenings, Baku wore a holiday appearance. Artistic triumphal arches and beautiful decorations filled the streets. Throughout the day, the delegates moved about the streets. Comrade Zinoviev was the object of much attention. Wherever he was seen in the streets, he was surrounded by cheering crowds.

By 1922, the Soviet Foreign Ministry acknowledged that in the East the influence of the Soviets was 'constantly growing' because of its diplomatic creativity (examples for them were the 1921 Soviet-Turkish treaty and the 1921 Soviet-Persian Treaty).

The Communist International struggled to balance the needs of its European members with the members from the countries colonized by Europe. The former represented the countries of the colonizers. They had to fight in their own societies to build organizations of the working class and other allied classes at the same time as they were charged with driving an anti-colonial agenda. The Comintern's attempt to get them to hold a Colonial Conference spluttered. It was difficult to find out what these European communists – seen as a pipeline to the colonies – were doing in terms of practical work to build alliances between workers in their countries and in the colonies. These European communists found it difficult to work amongst workers in their countries who had been dominated by a labour aristocracy that was often pro-imperialist. It was not easy to push a double agenda – for the rights of the European workers and for the workers and peasants in the colonies. No such difficulty lay in the colonies – from Indo-China to the Gold Coast of Africa. But other difficulties haunted communists in the colonies. They found it difficult to create a precise framework to work with the bourgeois nationalists who also hated colonial rule but who had no problem with capitalism. These contradictions dampened the work of the Comintern. Nonetheless, it was through the Comintern that trade unionists and revolutionary nationalists from one end of the world found out about the work of their peers on the other side. The infrastructure of global communism was created by the Comintern activists, who travelled from one end of China to the other end of Mexico to meet with socialists, anarchists, syndicalists, rebels of all kinds to urge them towards unity with the Communist movement.

Papers such as *The Negro Worker* allowed unionists across the continents to keep up with each other and to experience the unity that allowed them to magnify their work. The Trinidadian Marxist intellectual C.L.R. James observed the work of his Trinidadian friend George Padmore, head of the International Trade Union Committee of Negro Workers. 'It must be remembered that men in Mombasa, in Lagos, in Fyzabad, in Port-au-Prince, in Dakar, struggling to establish a trade union or political organization, most often under illegal conditions and under heavy persecution, read and followed with exceptional concern the directives which came from the revered and trusted centre in Moscow', James wrote. This 'trusted centre' was the Comintern. It provided the necessary organization to help workers from one end of the world to be in touch with others at the other end. Padmore edited *The Negro Worker*, which gave 'hundreds of thousands of active Negroes and the millions whom they represented' access to the world, wrote James. It gave them insight into 'Communism in theory and the concrete idea of Russia as a great power, which was on the side of the oppressed'. This, James wrote even as he was critical of the USSR, 'is what *The Negro Worker* gave to the sweating and struggling thousands in the West Indies, in Nigeria, in South Africa, all over the world'.

Platforms such as Internationale Arbeiterhilfe (Workers' International Relief – IAH) emerged initially to help draw attention to the struggles inside the USSR with hunger – to enable Europeans mainly raise funds to help prevent famine. But the work of the IAH would eventually widen outwards, building solidarity campaigns from Japan to Mexico, from Argentina to Australia.

The IAH worked from Germany, but turned its energy outwards towards the 'oppressed and exploited' peoples of the world. It enabled communists and their allies to forge connections across continents and deepened the relations of radicals within their own countries. It allowed words like 'solidarity' to take on a tangible meaning. This would not have been possible without the active support of Moscow.

From one end of the planet to the other, Comintern agents such as Mikhail Borodin carried instructions and methods, wondering how best to help along the revolutions. Alongside them were men and women of the colonies who came to Moscow, studied revolutionary theory and then found their way back home to build communist parties against all odds. These people led colourful lives, dangerous lives, going from factory gate to printer's shop, from prison to exile. Their journeys were unpredictable – the Indian revolutionary M.N. Roy becomes a founder of the Mexican Communist Party, while the Chilean socialist Luis Emilio Recabarren becomes a founder of the Argentinian Communist Party. Dada Amir Haidar Khan (1900-89) leaves his remote village in Rawalpindi for the merchant marine, becomes an activist of the American Communist Party and then goes to the USSR to train at the University of the Toilers of the East, which sends him to India. Yusuf Salman Yusuf (1901-49) – known as Fahd – met a Comintern agent Piotr Vasili who helps him go to the University of the Toilers of the East, which sends him back to Iraq after a sojourn in Europe. Tan Malaka (1897-1949), who leaves the Dutch East Indies to study in Holland, returns to become a popular educator and communist, finds himself in exile and then in Moscow for the Fourth World Congress of the Comintern. Hồ Chí Minh (1890-1969), meanwhile, works on the ships and the hotels in France, the United States and on the Atlantic Ocean. He becomes a founder of the French Communist Party, goes to the USSR to study at the University of the Toilers of the East and then returns to Indo-China to lead his country to revolution. Each of them was born close to 1900 and each lead a colourful life, marked by the October Revolution which occurred in their teens. These were the people who lived along the circuits of the Comintern, for whom the USSR was a crucial node to develop their own ideas and to build their own revolutionary theories and networks.

In June 1917, Mirsaid Sultan-Galiev of Bashkiria, who had been secretary of the All-Russia Muslim Council, described why he had joined the Bolshevik party:

> Only they are striving to transfer the nationalities' fates into their own hands. Only they revealed who started the world war. What doesn't lead me to them? They also declared war on English imperialism, which oppresses India, Egypt, Afghanistan, Persia and Arabia. They are also the ones who raised arms against French imperialism, which enslaves Morocco, Algeria and other Arab states of Africa. How could I not go with them? You see, they uttered the words that have never been uttered before in the history of the Russian state. Appealing to all Muslims of Russia and the East, they announced that Istanbul must be in Muslims' hands.

Sultan-Galiev's words resonated not only from his native Bashkiria to the outer reaches of the Uzbek homelands but also in India, where tens of thousands of Indian *Muhajirs* sought to head out towards Istanbul to defend the Caliphate of the Ottoman Empire. These pan-Islamists ran into news of the USSR. In Kabul, Abdur Rab Peshawari told them, 'in Russia, a revolution had taken place and if we went there we could see and learn many things'. When a group arrived in Termez (in today's Uzbekistan), 'Red Army soldiers and officers came with a band, playing music to welcome' them. The Commander of the fort in the town told them to 'see how the Soviet country had changed after the revolution'. In Tashkent, these men who came to fight for pan-Islamism 'used to refer to themselves as Communists'. 'Several of these young *muhajirs* decided to go to the Soviet Union', writes the communist leader Muzaffar Ahmad, 'the land of revolution, rather than Turkey'. Seventeen students went to the University of the Toilers of the East in Moscow, while others studied in Tashkent at the Indian Military School ('one of us was taught to fly an aeroplane'). 'We had left our country once', wrote Ahmad. 'But after joining the Communist Party we were again anxious to return home'. They returned in pairs via Iran.

The connection between communism and pan-Islamism played an important role in this period. In 1922, Indonesia's Tan Malaka put this point explicitly,

> Alongside the crescent, the star of the Soviets will be the great battle emblem of approximately 250 million Muslims of the Sahara, Arabia, Hindustan and our Indies. Let us realize that the millions of proletarian Muslims are as little attracted to an imperialist pan-Islamism as to Western imperialism.

This was written in September. The next month, Tan Malaka was busy with the preparations for the Fourth Congress of the Comintern. He proposed that the Comintern should take up the issue of closer collaboration between pan-Islamism and Communism. His proposal was struck down. There was uneasiness for fairly obvious reasons, mostly to do with the very conservative tone struck by the Muslim clerics which resulted in their class alliance with the reactionary forces in their societies. There was no room in the debate to consider the more robustly anti-imperialist clergy, which was also not always keen on the feudal social patterns. These would be the old networks enlivened by Jamal al-din al-Afghani, the iterant anti-imperialist activist of the 19th century. Tan Malaka knew of those people and of Sarekat Islam (the Islamists Trade Union) in the Dutch East Indies, which would – for a while – be an important ally of the Indonesian Communist Party.

For these revolutionaries, from India to Khiva, colonialism

was an abomination. They longed for a world of freedom, where the workers and peasants would be in command of their destiny. Sultan-Galiev warned that the new USSR should not 'replace one class of European society by the world dictatorship of its adversary – that is, by another class from this same society'. Such a swap would 'bring no significant change in the situation of the oppressed part of humanity'. The USSR had to properly forge an anti-colonial and anti-racist future. Otherwise, it would slip into old habits of colonialism. 'In order to prevent the oppression of the toiler of the East', Sultan-Galiev said in 1918, 'we must unite the Muslim masses in a communist movement that will be our own and autonomous'. This was a lesson that many Russians could not learn. It is what Lenin feared. It is what became the basis of decades of struggle between the capitals of Soviet Asia and Soviet Europe.

Cavalry detachment of the Red Army in Mongolia (1919).

Enemy of Imperialism

The October Revolution and the communist movement appealed to people because, as the Comintern put it in 1928, 'they see in it the most decisive enemy of imperialism'. But, as the Comintern worried, the communist movement is not merely about an end to colonial domination. It was pledged to end imperialism, which by necessity meant to end the class domination of the peoples of the colonies by both the bourgeoisie in Europe and by the tropical bourgeoisie.

Lenin and the Bolsheviks understood vacillation. The February revolution of the workers and the peasants had overthrown the Tsar's regime. The government of Alexander Kerensky that followed was entangled in the tentacles of Russian capitalism and, through them, imperialism. The Russian capitalists had a subordinate position *vis-à-vis* imperialism. In his history of the Russian Revolution, Leon Trotsky wrote that the Russian autocracy on the one hand and the Russian bourgeoisie on the other hand 'contained features of compradorism, ever more and more clearly expressed. They lived and nourished themselves upon their connections with foreign imperialism, served it, and without their support could not have survived'. Trotsky used a word that was commonplace in radical circles at that time – compradorism. It comes from the days of Portugal's dominance in the ports of Asia. A 'comprador' was a buyer who came from an Asian society, lived in the port, bought goods for the Portuguese to their benefit and held these goods till Portuguese ships arrived to load them for their trading advantage. Marxists in Asia drew upon this word and used it to refer to the parasitical native bourgeoisie, which operated not for its own benefit alone but for the benefit *ultimately* of imperialism. The Russian bourgeoisie – like that of other bourgeois formations in the colonial and semi-colonial world – tended to the interests of imperialism more perhaps than the interests of themselves.

The Russian bourgeoisie was the host to European imperialism inside Russia, but, at the same time, the Russian bourgeoisie had its own imperial projects in Manchuria, Mongolia and Persia. Since Kerensky would not confront the Russian bourgeoisie and was willing to surrender to Western imperialism, his government would eventually betray the revolution. That it is why it had to be overthrown in October 1917. It is also what allowed the Bolsheviks to learn a lesson when they went into the anti-colonial struggle. The national bourgeoisie of the colonies would instinctively be against colonial rule, but they would not necessarily be against imperialism. Their class betrayal had to be confronted within the national movements.

The leadership of the nationalist anti-colonial movements did not necessarily have the will to stay the course. 'Many of these adherents of the Party, in the course of the revolutionary struggle, will reach a proletarian class point of view', the Comintern noted, but 'another part will find it more difficult to free themselves to the end, from the moods, waverings and half-hearted ideology of the petty bourgeoisie'. The nationalist bourgeoisie would dither like Kerensky's government, eager for some dignity as an independent nation, but also unwilling to fight for full freedom against the powerful imperialist bloc.

In the Comintern, the position against the national bourgeoisie was articulated firmly by the Iranian Communist Avetis Sultan-Zade, who had joined the Bolshevik Party in 1912 in St. Petersburg, where he was then studying. After the revolution, Sultan-Zade went to Persia, where he worked to build the Communist movement in the northern region, and to Central Asia, where he worked amongst the Persian émigré workers. He joined the Adalat Party, a Persian party influenced by Marxism, which would eventually become the Communist Party of Persia. Sultan-Zade saw that even within his party there were people who were not committed to immediate land reform and were eager to collaborate with nationalists who had no articulated and well-developed social agenda. In the Comintern, where he had some influence, Sultan-Zade warned of the dangers of dissolving independent communist parties into the nationalist tide. Communists should centrally be involved in the nationalist movement, but they should also retain their organizational independence. 'The evolution of class struggle will, in the near future', Sultan-Zade said in November 1920, 'force the bourgeoisie even in the colonial countries to abandon all and every revolutionary idea'.

Sultan-Zade spoke from experience. From Moscow, where he had gone to work at the Executive Committee of the Comintern, he watched as nationalist leaders from Egypt to Turkey and in Persia cracked down on the communists, sending them to prison or to the gallows. He had an ally in M.N. Roy, who was also sceptical about the national bourgeoisie in the anti-colonial struggle. In 1924, Saad Zaghloul Pasha became Prime Minister of Egypt and arrested the entire central committee of the Egyptian Communist Party, which had fought alongside Zaghloul's Wafd Party against British imperialism in the 1919 uprising. When Reza Khan came to power in Persia in 1925, he also arrested the Communist leadership of the Persian party and destroyed the party. In Turkey, Kemal Ataturk benefited from Soviet aid and Communist backing, but when he consolidated power by 1922 he suppressed his former Communist allies.

Nothing was as dramatic as the events in China, however, where the nationalist Kuomintang (KMT) massacred the Communists in 1927. The KMT wanted close relations with Moscow, eagerly sending its representative Hu Hanmin to the Comintern to beg for entry. Hu Hanmin cleverly suggested that he came from the 'revolutionary wing of the Kuomintang' and needed Comintern help to hold back the reactionaries. The Chinese Communist

Party, he told Moscow, was not necessary. The Comintern should merely build up the KMT's left flank. This the Comintern refused to do, although the USSR did provide considerable backing to the KMT as it built up its forces. The Communist Party was far too small to absorb all of the Comintern's energy. In September 1926, the KMT sent Shao Lizi – a journalist who had studied Marxism in the 1910s with Chen Duxiu – founder of the Chinese Communist Party. Shao Lizi tried to curry favour in Moscow, but he too failed. The USSR would help the KMT, but it was not prepared to call for the dissolution of the Communist Party. It was the KMT's betrayal of the communists in April 1927 that ended this dance between the KMT and the Comintern.

Should the Comintern have instructed the Chinese communists to stay away from the KMT after the founding of the Chinese Communist Party in 1921? The basis for united actions by all nationalist sections against imperialism was laid out by Lenin in 1916, 'The main thing *today* is to stand against the united, aligned front of the imperialist powers, the imperialist bourgeoisie and the social-imperialists, and for the utilization of *all* nationalist movements against imperialism for the purposes of the socialist revolution.' The goal remained the 'social revolution', but the weakness of the working class required an alliance with all classes in the national struggle. The Soviets understood fully the power of imperialism. Right after the October Revolution, *every* imperialist power – from the United Kingdom to the United States – sent arms, equipment and encouragement to the White Armies to go in and overthrow the workers' state. Neither of the White forces led by Admiral Alexander Kolchak nor General Anton Denikin would have been able to sustain their war without imperialist assistance. No peasant – now given land by the Soviets – was willing to fight for free to restore the aristocrats to power. Winston Churchill, an influential person in the British government, said that 'one might as well legalize sodomy as recognize the Bolsheviks'. His was a fanatical view against communism. Others did not entirely oppose him. What stopped them was the exhaustion of the British exchequer and that of the other imperialist powers by the Great War. The imperialist invasion of the USSR was not a form of dialogue or an export of democracy. This was an armed action against the new government. Imperialism's brutality had been on display across the continents, from the barbarism of the Belgians in the Congo to the harsh treatment by the Italians against the Libyans in 1911 and by the British, Dutch and French from the Caribbean to South-East Asia. It was against this force that Lenin cautioned unity of all national classes.

Lenin warned that if the communists did build the confidence of the people, then they would only weaken any popular unity against imperialist intervention. In the anti-colonial struggles, the communists had to be with the people. That was paramount. But to be with the people did not mean to adopt a populist politics – to be the ventriloquists' dummy that says whatever social views the people hold. The communists must both hold to their values, but must not allow these values to be too far from the common sense of the people. This was a tricky business and required deftness and tact. It was why Lenin warned the Mongolian People's Party – in November 1921 – to desist from changing their name to a communist party. The Party, he said, could not be ahead of the general consciousness of the people. When the proletariat develops its confidence and begins to shape the popular movement, only then should the People's Party become a Communist Party. 'A mere change of signboards is harmful and dangerous', Lenin told a Mongolian delegation. The Mongolians had already made their revolution in July of that year. Three years later, in 1924, the newly named Mongolian People's Revolutionary Party would join the Comintern. The use of the word *revolutionary* substituted for the word *communist*.

The Mongolians wanted space to produce their own revolutionary theory and policies. But their reliance on the Soviets for material aid was entangled with their reliance upon Soviet policy for their own development – all in fear of the intervention of imperialism, which was not unfounded (as the invasion by Baron Roman von Ungern-Sternberg in 1921 was to show). Ulaanbaatar's reliance upon the Kremlin seriously narrowed the ability of its revolutionary movement to build on its own history and to build its own capacity for socialist theory and practice. Narrow views of development led to a distortion of the pastoral economy, which undermined the ability of the herders to tend to their animals. Mass migration to China, as well as a revolt in 1931-32, was the obvious outcome. Another was the centralization of rule under Khorloogiin Choibalsan, who took his lead from Moscow and not from Mongolian history.

Just a handful of years after the Mongolians had come to see Lenin, Tan Malaka wrote bitterly about the Comintern's too firm hand on the levers of revolutionary politics in China and in the Dutch East Indies,

> The Moscow leadership is good only for Russia. With examples from Germany, Italy and Bulgaria, it is demonstrated that the Moscow leadership has failed for other countries. The entire Third International [Comintern] is built up in the Russian interest, and young Eastern leaders, in particular, will be inclined to go over to blind worship or lose their independence, with the result that they will lack contact with their own masses, who have different impulses from the Russian people.

When Tan Malaka was asked if this criticism of Moscow would bring him and the Indonesian communists towards the Fourth International of Leon Trotsky, then in the middle of a struggle against Joseph Stalin, he responded, 'The people of the Indies have enough to do without waiting around for the conclusion of the fight between Stalin and Trotsky.' This was the attitude in most of the anti-colonial countries. Individuals certainly admired Trotsky for his role in the October Revolution and for his work building the Red Army, and some even agreed with his criticism of the USSR's tendency towards bureaucracy. However, this was not enough for them to break with the USSR, which provided an important inspiration and necessary resources for their own movements. Trotskyism had very little impact on the Third World – except in Sri Lanka, in Bolivia and Argentina as well as amongst small numbers of intellectuals. Trotskyism's denunciation of the anti-colonial national states (those who formed the Non-Aligned Movement) and then the Cuban Revolution alienated it from the communists in the Third World.

Anti-colonial nationalism could not easily be denounced. Lenin recognized that it was a 'difficult task' to navigate the shoals of anti-colonial nationalism. Such a problem had to be dealt with carefully. There was 'no communist booklet' that had the answers for the radicals in the anti-colonial movements. They would have to throw themselves into the struggle and find their answers there. Sometimes movements did. At other times, they looked for impossible formulas.

José Carlos Mariátegui (1894-1930).

Eastern Marxism

Only at the end of his life did Karl Marx leave the shores of Europe and travel to a country under colonial dominion. This was when he went to Algeria in 1882. 'For Mussalmans, there is no such thing as subordination', Marx wrote to his daughter Laura Lafargue. Inequality is an abomination to 'a true Mussalman', but these sentiments, Marx felt, 'will go to rack and ruin without a revolutionary movement'. A movement of revolutionary understanding would easily be able to grow where there was this cultural feeling against inequality. Marx did not write more about Algeria or about Islam. These were observations made by a father to his daughter. But they do tell us a great deal about Marx's sensibility.

There was no room in Marxism for the idea that certain people needed to be ruled because they were racial or social inferiors. In fact, Marxism – from Marx's early writings onward – always understood human freedom as a universal objective. Human slavery and the degradation of human beings into wage slavery awoke in Marx his prophetic indignation. One of Marx's most famous passages in *Capital* (1867) pointed out that the 'rosy dawn of the era of capitalist production' should not be found in the antiseptic bank or factory. The origin of capitalism had to be found – among other processes – in 'the extirpation, enslavement and entombment in mines of the aboriginal population, the beginning of the conquest and looting of the East Indies, the turning of Africa into a warren for the commercial hunting of Black skins'. Capitalism grew and was sustained by the degradation of humanity. No wonder, then, that anti-colonialism would play such an important role in the Marxist movement.

When Marxism travelled outside the domain where Marx first developed the theory, it had to engage with what Lenin called 'the most essential thing in Marxism, the living soul of Marxism, the concrete analysis of concrete conditions'. This formula was valuable from the Dutch East Indies to the Andes.

In the Andes (in South America), one of the greatest (and least known) Marxist thinkers – José Carlos Mariátegui (1894-1930) – wrote in 1928, 'We do not wish that Socialism in America be a tracing and a copy. It must be a heroic creation. We must, with our own reality, in our own language, bring Indoamerican socialism to life.' What did Mariátegui do? He read his Marx and his Lenin – and he studied deeply in the social reality of the Andes. Lenin's theory of the worker-peasant alliance provided a fundamental addition to his Marxism. The 'socialist revolution in a mainly agrarian country like Peru in the 1920s', he wrote, 'was simply inconceivable without taking into consideration the insurgent mobilization of indigenous rural communities that were challenging the power of large land-owners (*latifundistas*) who were responsible for keeping alive old forms of economic exploitation'. The agent of change in Peru amongst the producing classes had to include the indigenous rural communities whose population was mainly Amerindian. To seek the insurgents amongst the minuscule industrial sector of Lima alone would be to go into battle with capital with one hand tied behind the back. This is an echo of Lenin's call for worker and peasant unity, but with the indigenous communities now in the framework.

Were the indigenous rural communities capable of a socialist movement? In the 1920s, when Mariátegui was writing, the prevailing intellectual fashion with regard to the rural communities was *indigenismo*, or Indianness – meaning a cultural movement that revived and celebrated Amerindian cultural forms but did not seek to explore their transformative potential. *Indigenismo* defanged the Amerindians and romantically saw them as culture producers but not history producers. Mariátegui reinterpreted their history in a more vibrant way – looking backwards at Inca primitive socialism and current struggles against the *latifundistas* as resources for social transformation. 'The thesis of a communist Inca tradition is', he wrote, 'the defence of a historical continuity between the ancient Inca communal way of life and the Peruvian communist society of the future'. Mariátegui's Andean socialism was never a restoration of the past, of a primitive communism of an ancient Inca world. 'It is clear that we are concerned less with what is dead than with has survived of the Inca civilization', he wrote in 1928. 'Peru's past interests us to the extent it can explain Peru's present. Constructive generations think of the past as an origin, never as a programme'. In other words, the past is a resource not a destination – it reminds us of what is possible, and its traces show us that elements of that old communitarianism can be harnessed in the fight against colonial private property relations in the present. When Marxism came to the Third World, it had to be supple and precise – learn from its context, understand the way capitalism morphs in a new venue and explore the ways for social transformation to drive history.

The Comintern tried to be supple, but its limited knowledge of the world meant it ended up being far too dogmatic to be always useful. By the late 1920s, the Comintern suggested the creation of a Black Belt in the southern region of the United States, Native Republics in South Africa and an Indian Republic along the Andean region of South America. From Moscow, it appeared as if the nationalities theory could be easily transported to these distant lands. For South America, the theory was debated at the First Latin American Communist Conference held in Buenos Aires in June 1929. Fierce debate broke out here, with the Comintern's preferred position being opposed by Mariátegui's associates. 'The construction of an autonomous state from the Indian race', Mariátegui wrote, 'would not lead to the dictatorship of the Indian proletariat, nor much less the formation of an Indian State without classes.' What would be created is an 'Indian bourgeois State with all of the internal and external contradictions of other bourgeois states'. The preferred option would be of the 'revolutionary class movement of the exploited indigenous masses', which was the only way for them to 'open a path to the true liberation of their race'. The debate on goals and strategy became so fierce that this was the only Latin American Communist Conference to be held. 'The indigenous proletariat await their Lenin', Mariátegui wrote. He meant not a Lenin as such, but a theory that could emerge from the movements to lead them against the rigid structures of the past and present.

This was not always the lesson that was learned. But it is our lesson now.

E.M.S. Namboodiripad (1909-98) was born a decade after Mariátegui and outlived him by many decades. He was not only an innovative Marxist but also the leader of the Communist movement in India. From his 1939 report to the Malabar Tenancy Enquiry Committee to his 1970s essays on caste and class, EMS explored the Marxist method to interpret the history and society of India. For historical materialism – the historical narrative laid out by Marx – society moved through two stages, from slavery to feudalism, and then from feudalism to capitalism, in anticipation of a future stage, from capitalism to socialism. Nothing like this happened in India. 'India remained tied to the same old order', EMS wrote, 'under which the overwhelming majority of the people belonged to the oppressed and backward castes. This is the essence of what Marx called India's *unchanging* society where the village was not touched by the wars and upheavals at the higher levels'. Caste society and the hegemony of Brahmanism had a most pernicious impact on Indian society. The caste system not only kept the oppressed masses in thrall, the ideological hegemony of Brahmanism resulted in a sustained stagnation of science and technology, and, therefore, ultimately, of the productive forces as well. This process weakened India, leaving the door wide open for European colonialism. As EMS put it, 'the defeat of the oppressed castes at the hands of the Brahmanic overlordship, of materialism by idealism, constituted the beginning of the fall of India's civilization and culture which in the end led to the loss of national independence.'

The stagnation of Indian history from the time of Adi Shankara in the 8th century was encapsulated in the caste-based feudal society. This caste order with its religious justifications was able to contain its contradictions. This meant that while challenges to the caste order by rebellion did occur across Indian history, none of these rebellions were able to frontally assault caste and break caste hierarchy in any substantive way. Neither British colonialism nor the Indian bourgeoisie in the post-colonial state had any real appetite to smash caste. The conversion of feudal landlords into capitalist landlords and the conversion of tenant serfs into the agrarian proletariat did not break the back of feudalism. The transformations merely superimposed capitalist social relations upon the caste-based feudal order. 'In India', EMS wrote, 'many of the forms of exploitation of the pre-capitalist system are continuing, some in the original and some in changed forms. There exists along with these a new system of exploitation as a result of capitalist development'. The agrarian proletariat, because of the old feudal relations, experienced harsh pauperization – the poor in the fields got poorer – as old feudal customs allowed landlords to transfer all the burdens of agriculture on their workers while reaping all the profits – little of it re-invested to modernize agriculture in any way.

Pre-capitalist social formations cultivated by colonialism and by the national bourgeoisie had to be systematically undermined by the people's movements of independent India. EMS traced the potentialities within Indian society, finding opportunities for social progress and brakes against it. Cognizant of the special oppression of caste and of religious majoritarianism in Indian society, EMS fought against the organizing of people based on these very lines; one cannot fight caste oppression on caste lines. Instead, caste oppression had to be fought by organizing people into unified class organizations that understood and emphasized the special role of caste in Indian society. As he put it in his essay on caste and class,

> We had then and still have to fight a two-front battle. Ranged against us on the one hand are those who denounce us for our alleged 'departure from the principles of nationalism and socialism', since we are championing 'sectarian' causes like those of the oppressed castes and religious minorities. On the other hand are those who, in the name of defending the oppressed caste masses, in fact, isolate them from the mainstream of the united struggle of the working people irrespective of caste, communities and so on.

But the tonic of unity was not meant to dissolve questions of social indignity experienced by oppressed castes, by women, by *Adivasis*, by those who experienced the violence of class hierarchy alongside the violence of other hierarchies. These questions had to be at the table. It took the Communist movement in India many decades to wrestle with the precise balance between the need for unity of all exploited people and for special emphasis on certain kinds of oppressions along lines of social division. The initial organizational route proposed by Indian communism was to use the platform of class organizations to openly attack caste oppression, religious majoritarianism and feudal male chauvinism. But soon it became clear that this was insufficient.

The working class is not made up of unmarked bodies of workers. It is made up of people with experiences of social hierarchies and indignity who require particular emphasis to fight those hierarchies. This is why Indian communism would eventually develop organizational platforms – such as the All-India Democratic Women's Association (AIDWA) and the Tamil Nadu Untouchability Eradication Front – that would concentrate attention on the specific hierarchies that needed to be combatted alongside the class demands of the Left. The point is made clearly by Brinda Karat, a leader of the CPI (M) and a former President of AIDWA,

A mechanical understanding of class is often problematic. When Marx said, workers of the world unite he was not speaking of male workers. We are unable to integrate the multiple forms of the double burden that working women face as an integral part of our struggle. All successful revolutions have shown the critical role of working women in the revolution. We know the February revolution in Russia was started by the huge street demonstrations of women workers. Apart from gender, in our experience in India, within the working classes, there are sections which face added oppression and discrimination on the basis of caste, with a large section of the so-called untouchables, the Dalits, relegated to the lowest rungs of the social ladder. Caste acts as an instrument for the intensification of the extraction of surplus value of the Dalits. Somewhat similar is the assault on the rights of *Adivasi* communities (tribal communities) with the corporate grab of land, forests, destruction of histories, cultures, languages, and ways of life. No class struggle in India can succeed without at the same time challenging the birth-based hierarchical caste system against Dalits or the specific issues that *Adivasi* workers face. I think this would be equally relevant to the question of race, religious-based discrimination or even against immigrants in other countries. These aspects have grown in the last century and working-class struggles which ignore these aspects damage and weaken themselves laying themselves open to legitimate charges of being racist or casteist. Thus class consciousness must necessarily include the consciousness of the specific exploitation that workers may face because of their caste or racial origins or because of their gender.

Naciye Hanim at the Congress of the Toilers of the East, Baku (1920).
Courtesy: La Chaux-de-Fonds Métropole Horlogère (Switzerland).

To See the Dawn

It could not have been easy for the Turkish communist Naciye Hanim, a teacher from Istanbul, to stand up in the Congress of the People of the East in 1920. The meeting was in Baku, which had established itself – along with Tashkent – as one of the hubs for Eastern communism. Hanim was one of the few women at the Congress, despite the efforts of the Comintern leadership. There were only 55 female delegates in the room of 2,000 delegates. Nonetheless, the Comintern ensured that two women took their seats alongside two men as joint chairs and three women won election to the presidium. Women need to overcome the 'despotism of men', the delegates were told by the Comintern representatives, as much as the despotism of capital. It was a firm message to a room of people who were not entirely eager to agree.

Hanim warned the delegates that 'however sincere and however vigorous your endeavours may be, they will be fruitless unless you summon the women to become real helpers in your work'. She did not mollify her views. 'People who view the fact that women are making up with their labour for the shortage of beasts of burden as contributing to the cause of equal rights for women are unworthy of our attention.' Many in the hall would have been stung by her comments, if they bothered to listen.

The organizers placed Hanim's speech on the last day. It was late. People were restless, eager to go home. 'Many violent speeches were made', wrote the British informer, 'but the general effect was in many cases spoiled by large numbers of Moslem representatives going outside to say their prayers'. A delegate warned – along the grain of Hanim's warning – that 'we were not able to immediately form all our customs and conditions of life into a communist framework'. The East, he said, is 'completely different, its interests are completely different, from the West'. The West was not so different, as the Bolshevik leader Alexandra Kollontai had been suggesting in her many writings on the importance of women's emancipation. But the East was no paradise, as Hanim made clear.

Hanim's list of demands bears consideration, for it could very well be a radical list even today:

Complete equality of rights.

Ensuring to women unconditional access to educational and vocational institutions established for men.

Equality of rights of both parties in marriage.

Unconditional abolition of polygamy.

Unconditional admission of women to employment in legislative and administrative institutions.

Establishment of committees for the rights and protection of women everywhere, in cities, in towns, and villages.

Hanim was not an idealist. She took life by the throat and demanded more of it. 'True, we may stumble in pathless darkness, we may stand on the brink of yawning chasms,' she closed her comments lyrically, 'but we are not afraid, because we know that in order to see the dawn one has to pass through the dark night.'

Hanim had allies in Moscow, particularly in the Zhenotdel (women's department). The year after the Baku conference in 1920, Alexandra Kollontai, then head of the Zhenotdel, wanted to convene a Congress of Eastern Women to put demands such as Hanim's on the table for Soviet policy. At the Second International Conference of Communist Women held in Moscow from June 9 to 14, 1921, the discussion on 'Eastern women' was vibrant. The Conference's final resolution called upon the Party and all state institutions in the Soviet East to 'wage a struggle against all prejudices, moral and religious customs oppressive to women, conducting this agitation likewise among men'. The main instrument to raise the 'cultural level of the populace' would be to fight to build unions of women – 'clubs of women workers', where the 'clubs must be centres of cultural enlightenment – institutions that demonstrate through experience what women can achieve through their own initiative for their emancipation (the organization of nurseries, kindergartens, literacy schools under the auspices of the clubs, etc.)'. In the Soviet East, the proletarian women must be organized into trade unions and unions of housewives, as well as be given the courage to fight for the implementation of equal rights enshrined in Soviet legislation. 'The particulars of everyday life of the peoples of the East' must be respected, noted the resolution. This meant that the struggles must not be conducted in a racist and self-righteous way but must put the women of the East at the forefront to fight for a revolution of their own cultural worlds.

Kollontai, as head of the Zhenotdel, along with Lenin and Alexander Shlyapnikov felt that the conclusions of the Second Conference of Communist Women suggested the need for a special Congress of Eastern Women. After an acrimonious politburo meeting in August 1921, which raised the issue of this Congress but then voted against it, Kollontai reproached Lenin about the disorganization of the government and the negative effect this had on the Zhenotdel. Kollontai wrote of her frustration, 'In the winter we planned three times to have an Eastern Congress [of Women] and three times it was cancelled, in agreement with [the Organizational Bureau], and I was not informed, and Zhenotdel was not notified of the cancellation!' Kollontai felt hemmed in by the conservative views held by some members of the Soviet leadership. Stalin was particularly brusque. When asked about the need for a Congress of Eastern Women, Stalin said, 'What for? Why drag women of the veil here? We will have too many problems to deal with. The husbands would protest. It's too early. Who wants their affairs to be examined?'

A Conference of Eastern Women was, nonetheless, held. It

Alexandra Kollontai surrounded by women from the Soviet East (1921).

was mainly about women in the Soviet East. The Conference's sense was that 'work among Turkic women to date has not been sufficiently developed'. Local party committees were asked to focus their 'serious attention' on work amongst women. The Conference suggested that women of the East must be organized into trade unions and into various clubs. The main point raised by Kollontai, by Hanifi Burnashev (a Tartar leader who was by then secretary of the Ferghana party) and by Mirsaid Sultan-Galiev was to work carefully amongst the people,

> Communist education of the women's masses by using all types of agitation and propaganda of the idea of communism and the practical participation of women in Soviet construction: all of these activities can be conducted successfully if representatives of the working people's masses themselves of the peoples of the East are recruited for the actual work. Women's departments must guide the work of young functionaries from among the communists of the Peoples of the East, while listening closely to all the practical recommendations they make on the basis of experience and knowledge of the milieu, as well as by helping to implement them.

In Central Asia as a consequence, local Bolsheviks set up local chapters of the Zhenotdel in Bukhara (1923) and Khiva (1924) as well as set up women's clubs in Ferghana (1925). In February 1925, the Presidium of the Central Executive Committee of the USSR affirmed the 'rights of women of the Soviet East'. In the Soviet East, the Zhenotdel's leadership moved a rigorous agenda against traditional forms of oppression, such as polygyny and women's seclusion. The struggle was not easy. The local parties and radicals – mostly comprising Central Asians – were caught between denouncing religious fanatics as well as ingrained customs, and facing a rebellion against Soviet policy led by the traditionalists.

Zhenotdel's leader Serafima Liubimova noted on May 19, 1926, that various traditional forms such as bride price, underage marriage and seclusion, needed to be made illegal. 'The way of life which has been preserved until now is women's slavery', she said, 'that is in contradiction to economics and hampers the movement among broad masses of women toward economic independence'. Liubimova wanted the various republics of Central Asia to pass laws that would forbid these practices. But laws – which did eventually come – were not sufficient. Social norms would not be entirely broken by new laws. Besides, as the Zhenotdel units found, women sometimes adopted these customary ways as a way to take comfort and power in familiar domestic settings. Conflicts between mullahs and jadids (elite reformers) did not ease the passage from older forms of domesticity to the newly available ways. The Soviets hesitated in the first decade, unwilling to directly confront Central Asian culture for fear of a widespread revolt in the region.

On March 8, 1927, on International Women's Day, Zhenotdel activists came out on the streets in the major Uzbek cities. The women marched through the streets to city squares, which had been decorated with red banners that carried militant slogans of women's liberation. Musicians greeted the women, who then sat on carpets to listen to their leadership attack old customs and celebrate communism as the path ahead. Some of the veiled women tore off their veil and burnt them. A new project – *hujum* (storming) – would be led by the Zhenotdel activists in a direct fight against hierarchical customs of Central Asia. This was an aggressive assault – *K nastupleniiu!* (To the attack!) – said the activists as they conducted direct actions as well as built women's institutions (clubs, schools). The Zhenotdel activists were now in direct confrontation with the clergy and with the landlords, who benefitted from the social quiet imposed by the old ways.

The reaction to the *hujum* was fierce but private. There were few public protests to defend the *yashmak* (veil) and illiteracy. The 'protests' were against the women who had spoken out or against women who tried to adopt the new norms. During this period of the late 1920s, the Uzbek Supreme Court noted that seventy-one cases came before them of men angry at women for their various assertions. The Court convicted 127 people for their aggression against the women. The Tashkent court dealt with thirty-eight cases of this kind; in thirteen of them, men killed women. In 1928, 270 Uzbek women were murdered for unveiling themselves. The Zhenotdel activists persisted. The *hujum* was not an easy fight nor did it succeed in fully transforming the cultural worlds of the nomadic Kazakh, Kyrgyz and Turkmen families. It would take decades for these ideas to seep into the generations.

The fight for women's education was equally difficult. In 1931, the Soviets surveyed the schools in Surkhan-Darya Oblast. In one village, not untypical, they found no girls in school. If education could be a way to move a new cultural agenda, it would not work if girls were not coming to school. Before the Revolution, the literacy rate for women in Central Asia was nearly zero. By 1970, it would be 99 per cent. The journey between 1917 and 1970 is something to behold. It took a great deal of effort by the local Zhenotdel activists, the local Communist Party workers and the Soviet state to push this agenda. Improved literacy rates simultaneously meant an improvement in health indicators. Patience was necessary, but so too perseverance. It was not possible to be conciliatory towards the old ways. These had to be disrupted. In 1964, at the 40th anniversary celebration of the Uzbek Soviet Socialist Republic, Fatima Kasymova took to the stage to talk about her life. Her story gives us a sense of Naciye Hanim's hopes,

> Should I tell you about my life as the head of the Engels collective farm in the Samarkand region for the past twenty years as a mother who, besides raising six children of her own, adopted ten children of different nationalities during World War II, that having graduated from Samarkand Agricultural Institute, I am now working on a Master's thesis on the selection of the new, very sweet variety of Sultana grapes. . . . My biography, the biography of an ordinary

Uzbek woman, would be a vivid example of what Soviet power has given to the women of the East.

Communist women outside the USSR took great inspiration from the positions taken by the Soviets and their struggles. It had become commonplace for communist parties across the world to create women's fronts by the 1930s to develop struggles led by women on women's issues. These organizations and the struggles that drew in women of all sectors shaped the issues that would be brought to the communist parties, which – being rooted in the world – would not easily adopt them. Women such as Aminah Rahhal and Naziha Jawdat Dulaymi of the Iraqi Communist Party and the League for the Defence of Women's Right as well as the Venezuelan communist Argelia Laya and Ecuadorean communist Tránsito Amaguaña ('Mama Tránsito') shaped this world of communist women's activism. Many of these women would form organizations that would become part of the Women's International Democratic Federation (WIDF), founded in Paris in 1945.

'The Covenant of White and Brown Will Make Humanity Free!' League Against Imperialism and Colonial Domination (1927). Courtesy: International Institute of Social History (Amsterdam).

Colonial Fascism

In 1950, Aimé Césaire, the communist from Martinique, one of the clearest voices of the 20th century, looked back at the long history of colonialism that was coming to an end. He wanted to judge colonialism from the ashes of Nazism, an ideology that surprised the innocent in Europe but which had been fostered slowly in Europe's colonial experience. After all, the instruments of Nazism - racial superiority as well as brutal, genocidal violence - had been cultivated in the colonial worlds of Africa, Asia and Latin America. Césaire, the effervescent poet and communist, had no problem with the encounter between cultures. The entanglements of Europe's culture with that of Africa and Asia had forged the best of human history across the Mediterranean Sea. But colonialism was not cultural contact. It was brutality.

> Between colonization and civilization there is an infinite distance; that out of all the colonial expeditions that have been undertaken, out of all the colonial statutes that have been drawn up, out of all the memoranda that have been dispatched by all the ministries, there could not come a single human value.

Césaire was adamant: colonialism had produced nothing that would earn it respect in the scales of history. This was in 1950, when a few nations had just emerged out of the scar of colonialism and when many societies fought pitched battles to extricate themselves from colonial power. What had come to define fascism inside Europe through the experience of the Nazis - the jackboots and the gas chambers - were familiar already in the colonies. This colonial fascism, Césaire argued in *Discourse on Colonialism*, needed to be emphasized. Colonialism was asserting itself in this period, pushing to revive its empires from Vietnam to Algeria, from Kenya to Malaya. It pretended to distinguish itself from fascism, then considered essentially evil, and to resurrect itself in a paternalist and benign form. Césaire would have nothing to do with that. Colonialism and fascism shared too much at the level of effects – in terms of how they appeared to their victims. It was clear to Césaire, as a Marxist, that fascism was a political form of bourgeois rule in times when democracy threatened capitalism; colonialism, on the other hand, was naked power justified by racism to seize resources from people who were not willing to hand them over. Their form was different but their manners were identical.

From the anti-colonial struggles of the Communist International and the League Against Imperialism to the anti-fascist struggle in Spain and then against the Nazi war machine, the Soviet Union acquitted itself well. The Soviets, like Césaire, saw the links between colonialism and fascism – both tied to each other inextricably by racism. It was not possible to fight fascism and collaborate with colonialism. The two emerged from the same origin, which the communist leader R.P. Dutt called *capitalist decay*. In his *Fascism and Social Decay* (1934), Dutt pointed out that the 'revolt against science' prepares the ground for 'all the quackeries and charlatanries, of chauvinism, racial theories, anti-semitism, Aryan grandmothers, mystic swastikas, divine missions, strong-man saviours, and all the rest of the nonsense through which alone capitalism today can try to maintain its hold a little longer'. Racism, the root of both colonialism and fascism, was not 'insane', Dutt wrote, but 'completely rational and calculated'. Capitalism cannot offer a 'rational defence' of itself, of the manner in which it creates and sustains social inequality. It, therefore, takes refuge on 'a wave of obscurantism, holding out fantastic symbols and painted substitutes for ideals'.

COLONIAL FASCISM

In 1917, the Soviets revealed the secret treaties of the imperialist powers. When he released these documents, Leon Trotsky – the People's Commissar of Foreign Affairs – noted, 'Secret diplomacy is a necessary weapon in the hands of the propertied minority which is compelled to deceive the majority in order to make the latter serve its interests. Imperialism, with its worldwide plans of annexation, its rapacious alliances and machinations, has developed the system of secret diplomacy to the highest degree'. The Soviet record against colonialism was clear, even as the Comintern struggled to produce a firm line in this or that country. There was no instance where the Soviets considered colonial rule to be worthwhile. The same with fascism, which the Soviets saw as anathema to humankind. Soviet aid to Republican Spain was one test and the other was the immense sacrifice of the USSR in the fight against fascism in World War II.

In 1931, the Spanish Left won the elections and inaugurated the Second Spanish Republic. An even more radical Popular Front government came to power in 1936. Only two countries, Mexico and the USSR – the two peasant republics that had been formed by revolutions – backed the Spanish Republic. Progressive policies to undercut landlords, the aristocrats and the capitalists set the Republic against the ruling bloc. That bloc would rapidly find solace in the fascist movement as well as in the army of General Francisco Franco that left Spanish colonized Morocco for the mainland. From North Africa, the fascists came into the Iberian Peninsula with the intent of overthrowing the Republic by force. A war ensued, which was – with the fascist Italian invasion of Ethiopia in 1935 – an early frontline of the fascist assault. The Soviets backed the Republic, as did Communist parties from around the world. Communists came to the aid of the Republic from the United States to the Philippines, from India to Ireland. The International Brigades, supported by the USSR, provided a bulwark against the onrush of the fascist armies, which were backed not only by the fascist powers (Italy and Germany) but also by the imperialist bloc (Britain and France). Fissures between the anarchists and the communists fractured the unities necessary in the fight against fascism, surely, but there it is undeniable that without logistical help – Operation X – from the Soviets the Republic would have been crushed immediately and not lasted until 1939.

When the Republic fell in March 1939, the imperialist and fascist blocs seemed fused. When Franco marched into Madrid, the British Ambassador went to greet him. When Nehru, who had been to the Republican front-lines and was fully behind the Republic, heard of this, he shuddered. This imperialist and fascist alliance was against humanity. Franco would remain in power until his death in 1975. He remained heralded by the 'democratic' countries of Europe.

The USSR, through the summer of 1939, faced the imminent threat of invasion by the fascist and imperialist powers. Such an invasion had taken place right after 1917. In the war in Spain, it became clear that Soviet armaments that went there through Operation X were not of the same quality as those produced by the Germans and the Italians. The Soviets sent 772 airmen in heavy Tupolev SB bombers, which turned out to be far slower and more vulnerable than the German Messerschmitt Bf 109. The Soviet army staff feared that an invasion by the Nazis and the imperialist bloc, after the fall of Spain, would be catastrophic for the USSR. The Nazis had already seized Austria in the Anschluss of 1938 and had threatened Lithuania with conquest in March 1939. The Italians had seized Albania in April 1939 and the two fascist powers – Italy and Germany – signed a decisive Pact of Steel in May 1939. Britain's appeasement of the fascist bloc at the Munich meeting in 1938 suggested collusion between the imperialist and the fascist bloc. This was the context of the Molotov-Ribbentrop Pact of August 1939, where the Soviets hoped to get some time to build up their capacity before an inevitable Nazi attack. Surely there should have been no compromise with fascism. But this was in the realm of realpolitik – a way to salvage time before the war that was to come. Indeed, in September 1939, the USSR opened nine factories to build aircraft and seven factories to build aircraft engines. The Red Army grew from 1 million (Spring of 1938) to 5 million (June 1941).

But Stalin had other ideas as well. On March 10, 1939, when the Spanish Republic was ready to fall, he said that the USSR should allow the 'warmongers to sink deeply into the mire of warfare, to quietly urge them on'. If Germany and Britain went to war, then it would 'weaken and exhaust' both allowing the USSR 'with fresh forces' to enter the fray eventually 'in the interest of peace to dictate terms to the weakened belligerents'. This would not happen. France was easily defeated by the Nazis and Britain could not find the way to bring troops to the European mainland. The war came to the USSR without the imperialists being weakened. The Nazis attacked the USSR as expected. The Soviets fought valiantly against the Nazis, losing over 26 million Soviet citizens in the long war that eventually destroyed the Nazi war machine.

It was the Soviet Union that saved the world from Nazism. It was Soviet armies that liberated most of the Nazi concentration camps, and it was the Soviet armies that entered Berlin and ended the war. General Dwight Eisenhower, the leading American soldier in the European sector, recalled his journey into the Eastern front after the end of the war, 'When we flew into Russia in 1945, I did not see a house standing between the western borders of the country and the area around Moscow. Through this overrun region, Marshal Zhukov told me, so many numbers of women, children and old men and been killed that the Russian Government would never be able to estimate the total.'

Fascism, to those in the colonized world, shared too much in its behaviour with colonialism: the racism surely but also the brutality and depravity, the oscillation between genocide and incarceration. Aimé Césaire did not see 'fascism' and 'colonialism' as separate endeavours. They were kin. But in Europe after 1945, there was a great push to see fascism as merely its European expression, an aberration of the Germans and the Italians. To suggest that fascism was merely Nazism with no linkage to colonialism allowed the Europeans and the North Americans to revive – without embarrassment – their colonial histories. The British used the full might of their armies to subdue national aspirations from Kenya to Malaya, while the French attempted to retake their old colonies from Indo-China to Algeria. The Dutch sent in their armies into Indonesia, while the Americans conducted coups and marine landings from Guatemala to the Dominican Republic and outwards to Iran.

In 1954, the US National Security Council's staff prepared an important memorandum on US policy towards Africa. The two main interests of the United States were its 'actual and potential US military bases in the area' and its 'access to, and utilization of, the strategic raw materials of the area'. To secure bases and raw materials the United States would need to 'support' the colonial powers' 'presence in the area' – namely to support the continuation of colonialism. US Secretary of State John Foster Dulles worried that decolonization would mean the delivery of the new states to the communists and so the loss to the US of bases and raw materials. 'Zeal' toward decolonization, he said, 'needs to be balanced by patience'. Here 'patience' simply meant the delay of decolonization. This was a return to the language and logic of imperialism from before World War II. There was no sense here that the anti-fascist struggle had any unity with the anti-colonial struggle, both part of the broader human struggle for freedom against tyranny. Fascism had been defeated, but colonialism was going to be welcomed into the post-war age.

In 1960, the US voted in the UN Political Committee against a resolution that called for Algerian independence. Later that year, the US voted – effectively – to allow no oversight into the Portuguese colonies in Africa. Finally, that year, the US abstained on a vote in the UN General Assembly for a 'Declaration on the Granting of Independence to Colonial Countries and Peoples'. This declaration was a significant feint by the USSR on behalf of the colonized world. During the 15th Session of the General Assembly on September 23, 1960, Nikita Khrushchev of the USSR said it was now time for 'the complete and final liberation of peoples languishing in colonial bondage'. In keeping with the UN Charter, the 100 million people still living under colonialism must be freed. Five days later, during the discussion over the Declaration, which was sponsored by the USSR, its representative to the UN Valerian Zorin called for independence for all colonial territories within a year. 'The process of liberation is irresistible and irreversible', noted the Declaration, which passed by 89 votes to 0, with nine abstentions (including colonial powers such as Belgium, France, Portugal, Spain, the United Kingdom and the apartheid state of South Africa). It was clear that the old colonial powers and the United States had little sympathy for the anti-colonial struggle, itself intertwined with the legacy of the October Revolution.

While Zorin made the case, along with 43 countries from Africa and Asia, in the United Nations, Cuba broke through its colonial domination into freedom. From the mountains of the Sierra Maestra and from the cities came the torrential power of the people against the US-backed dictator Fulgencio Batista. 'The revolution is made in the midst of danger', said Fidel Castro as he led his band of peasant-soldiers from the hills into the cities. They had triumphed against remarkable odds. Quickly, the revolutionaries passed a series of decrees – just as the Soviets had – to draw the key classes to their side. To draw in the urban Cubans, the revolutionaries cut rents by half – sending a strong signal to the bourgeoisie that they had a different class outlook. Then, the revolutionaries took on the United States, whose government held a monopoly over services to the island. Telephone and electrical companies – all American – were told to reduce their rates immediately. Then, on May 17, 1959, the Cuban government passed its agrarian reform – the keystone of the revolutionary process. Land holdings would be restricted so that no large landowners could dominate the landscape and so that the US sugar industry could not strangle the hopes of the island. The most radical part of the reform was not the land ceiling itself, but the logic that agrarian reform would transform the stagnation of the Cuban economy and its dependence upon the United States. The law clearly stated that, from a socialist standpoint,

> The agrarian reform has two principal objectives: (a) to facilitate the planting or the extension of new crops with the view of furnishing raw materials to industry, satisfying the food requirements of the nation, increasing the export of agricultural products and, reciprocally, the import of foreign products which are essential to use; (b) to develop the interior market (family, domestic) by raising the purchasing power of the rural population. In other words, increase the national demand in order to develop the industries atrophied by an overly restrained consumption, or in order to create those which, for lack of customers, were never able to get started among us.

The revolutionaries wanted to diversify their sugarcane island, produce food security for their people, remove people from desperation, increase the ability of people to consume a range of goods and engineer a people-centred rather than an export-centred economy. Long before Castro announced his commitment to communism, the regime had already developed a carefully thought out socialist platform.

The United States of America, having overthrown the radical nationalist government in Guatemala in 1954, was eager to repeat the task in Cuba in 1959. An embargo came swiftly, as did every form of humiliation possible against the Cuban people. The Cuban economy was structured around dependency to Washington, with the sugar bought by the US firms and with the island turned into a playground for American tourists. Now, the US decided to squeeze this little island, only ninety miles from the US shoreline. Gunboats were readied, a failed invasion tried in April 1961 at the Bay of Pigs. Cuba was vulnerable but also protected by the deep roots of its revolution. But would this protection be sufficient? Could Cuba, alone, be able to survive the onslaught from the United States?

On February 5, 1960, a leader in the USSR and an Old Bolshevik – Anastas Mikoyan – came to Havana to join Fidel Castro at the opening of a Soviet scientific, cultural and technical exhibition. A week later, Mikoyan and Castro signed an agreement for the USSR to buy Cuban sugar at the world market price (in dollars) and provide credits for the Cubans to buy Russian goods. The USSR would subsequently buy almost all the Cuban sugar harvest, even as the Russian consumer market could very well have been supplied by beet sugar from within the USSR. Prices fluctuated, but, on balance, the Cubans were able to find a regular buyer to take over from the United States. The Russians also provided over a $100 million in credits toward the construction of Cuba's chemical industry as well as trained Cuban technical and scientific workers in the USSR. Diversification of Cuba's economy remained on the cards, although it became clear that it would not be an easy task. In August 1963, Castro announced that diversification, as well as industrialization, would be postponed. Cuba needed to concentrate on its sugarcane harvest to earn the means to survive the embargo.

On February 24, 1965, Che Guevara addressed the Second Economic Seminar of Afro-Asian Solidarity in Algiers, Algeria. He had come to talk about the economic problems for a revolution in a post-colonial country. Overthrowing the former colonizer was not enough, Che said, since 'a real break' is needed from imperialism for the new state to actually flourish and not remain in dependency. How could the post-colonial state survive a hostile economic climate? Who would buy its goods – mainly primary, unprocessed goods – at a fair price, and who would lend it capital at fair terms to develop? Capitalist banks and countries would not provide the post-colonial state, particularly a socialist state, with the means to break out of the trap of underdevelopment. Banks would lend money to a post-colonial state at rates higher than

Castro joins in to harvest sugarcane (1969).

it would lend to a colonial power. Expensive money would only put the post-colonial state into further difficulty, as it would find it hard to service its debt and see its debt multiply out of hand. To prevent this situation, Che argued, the 'socialist countries must help pay for the development of countries now starting out on the road to liberation'. Trade between socialist countries must not take place based on the law of value of capitalism, but through the creation of fraternal prices. 'The real task', Che said, 'consists of setting prices that will permit development. A great shift in ideas will be involved in changing the order of international relations. Foreign trade should not determine policy, but should, on the contrary, be subordinated to a fraternal policy toward the peoples.'

China, in 1960, offered Cuba credit of $60 million without interest and without a timeline for repayment. This was an enviable loan. But the scale was much smaller than the Soviet assistance. By 1964, the USSR had provided Cuba with economic assistance valued at over $600 million, while the Eastern European countries offered several hundred million more in aid and assistance. The USSR had also trained over 3,000 Cubans in agronomy and agricultural mechanization as well as 900 Cubans as engineers and technicians. Che recognized the value of the Soviet 'fraternal policy' both in terms of the training and in the prices offered. 'Clearly, we could not ask the Socialist world to buy this quantity of sugar at this price based on economic motives', he had said in 1961, 'because really there is no reason in world commerce for this purchase and it was simply a political gesture'.

Dipa Nusantara Aidit, leader of the Communist Party of Indonesia, speaking at an election meeting in 1955. The Party would grow by leaps and bounds in the decade that followed.

Polycentric Communism

In 1956, Soviet tanks entered Hungary. Debate over this intervention spread across the world's left. 'The Polish and Hungarian people have written their critique of Stalinism upon the streets and squares', wrote the British Marxist E.P. Thompson. The Soviet intervention came a few months after the 20th Congress of the Communist Party of the USSR, where Nikita Khrushchev had denounced Stalin and blamed all distortions in the USSR on the 'cult of personality'. The attack on Stalin and the USSR's intervention in Hungary damaged its reputation in the Third World – a reputation secured not only because it had built a modern, equitable state out of a peasant society but also because it used its incredible prowess – built at great sacrifice – to defeat fascism. The anti-colonialism of the early Soviets was mirrored by the anti-fascism of the next generation. This was now damaged by the 20th-Congress revelations and by the invasion of Hungary.

Palmiro Togliatti, the leader of the Italian Communist Party, called for a reconsideration of the centrality of Moscow to the world communist movement. 'National roads to socialism' needed to be developed, Togliatti wrote, as he reiterated an older desire for 'polycentric communism'. This was to be a communism that was not centred around Moscow and Soviet foreign policy. The Soviet intervention in Hungary and the Khrushchev revelations produced in Europe a process that led – gradually – to the Eurocommunism of the Communist Party of Spain's leader Santiago Carrillo, who said, in 1976, 'once Moscow was our Rome, but no more. Now we acknowledge no guiding centre, no international discipline'. This was a communism that no longer believed in revolution but was quite satisfied with an evolutionary dynamic. The European parties, correct in their desire for the right to develop their own strategies and tactics, nonetheless, threw themselves onto a self-destructive path. Few remained standing after the USSR collapsed in 1991. They campaigned for polycentrism but, in the end, achieved only a return to social democracy.

Amongst the Third World communist parties, a different orientation became clear after 1956. While the Western European parties seemed eager to denigrate the USSR and its contributions, the parties in the Third World acknowledged the importance of the USSR but sought some distance from its political orientation. During their visits to Moscow in the 1960s, champions of 'African socialism' such as Modibo Keïta of Mali and Mamadou Dia of Senegal announced the necessity of non-alignment and the importance of nationally developed processes of socialist construction. Marshal Lin Biao spoke of the need for a 'creative application' of Marxism in the Chinese context. The young leader of the Indonesian Communist Party – Dipa Nusantara Aidit – moved his party towards a firm grounding in both Marxism-Leninism and the peculiarities of Indonesian history. In December 1961, Aidit told his party of the importance of 'polycentrism'. 'No Communist Party that is dependent upon another can develop normally', he said. In India, the Communist Party of India (Marxist) emerged out of the Communist Party of India in 1964 around a debate that included the role of the USSR as arbiter of national lines. 'We realize that we can learn very little from the experiences of the Soviet and the Chinese revolutions', said Hare Krishna Konar, a peasant leader of the CPIM. 'In the peculiar objective realities of India, we have to rely on ourselves to formulate the strategies and tactics of our revolution. The Indian peasant struggle must necessarily take a different tack from that of the CCP-led peasant struggle in China'.

In the Third World, where Communism was a dynamic movement, it was not treated as a religion that was incapable of error. 'Socialism is young', Che Guevara wrote in 1965, 'and has its mistakes.' Socialism required ceaseless criticism in order to strengthen it. Such an attitude was missing in Cold War Europe and North America, where the Cold Warriors of Capitalism took any self-criticism by the Communists for weakness and where the comrades tragically fell back upon defensiveness and the construction of illusions. 'The hidden hallmark of Western Marxism as a whole', wrote Perry Anderson in 1979, 'is thus that it is a politics of *defeat*.' This was not the attitude in the Third World where the Communist Party of the Soviet Union was seen as an ally but not as the hallmark of their revolutionary struggles. They did not link their movements in a theological way to the USSR. After 1956, Communism was penalized by the Cold Warriors for the Soviet intervention in Hungary. This played some role in the Third World, but it was not decisive. In India, in 1957 the Communists won an election in Kerala to become the ruling party in that state. In 1959, the Cuban revolution overthrew a dictatorship and adopted Marxism-Leninism as its general theory. In Vietnam, from 1954, the Communists took charge of the north of the country and valiantly fought to liberate the rest of their country. These were communist victories despite the intervention in Hungary.

In reaction to the developments in Hungary, the Communist Party of India's leader Ajoy Ghosh wrote a letter in *New Age* about these developments. He admitted that the party had been wrong in 'idealizing the USSR' and in not having been attentive to criticisms of the state. There was a violent debate in the Central Committee of the CPI over Hungary in December 1956, which was not easily resolved. The execution of Communist leader Imre Nagy in the summer of 1958 only turned more of the Indian communists against the direction being taken in the USSR. What was happening within the USSR?

A struggle opened up within the CPI over what should be the attitude of the party towards the USSR – with one section closer to the Soviet viewpoint and another taking a position against it.

In April 1957, at a meeting at the CPI's West Bengal provincial committee, the communists decided to disagree with the position that the USSR must be followed blindly. The committee resolved to 'interpret and apply' Marxism-Leninism for their own conditions. That July, CPI leader Z.A. Ahmed said that 'the USSR is no model now'. In October, at a closed meeting of the Bombay party committee, the party members strongly criticized the CPSU and the CPI's inability to be critical of the USSR. In June 1958, the West Bengal CPI unit told the party leadership that they disagreed with the party's position of subservience to the USSR. The execution of Nagy and the failure of the CPI to condemn it troubled these communists as did the CPI's break with Yugoslavia in concert with the USSR. When the CPI split in 1964, the new party that emerged from it – the Communist Party of India (Marxist) – respected the October Revolution and the Chinese Revolution, but took its orders from neither. It would develop its own theory, based on – as Lenin had said – 'the most essential thing in Marxism, the living soul of Marxism, the concrete analysis of concrete conditions'.

Much the same history propelled the Indonesian Communist Party (PKI) forward from 1951, when it had merely 5,000 members, to 1964, when it had two million party members and an additional fifteen million members in its mass organizations (half of them in the Indonesian Peasants' Front). The party had deep roots in the heavily populated sections of east and central Java but had – in the decade after 1951 – begun to make gains in the outer islands, such as Sumatra. A viciously anti-communist military was unable to stop the growth of the party. The new leadership from the 1953 Party Central Committee meeting were all in their thirties, with the new Secretary General – Aidit – merely thirty-one years old. These communists were committed to mass struggles and to mass campaigns, to building up the party base in rural Indonesia. The Indonesian Peasants' Front and the Plantation Workers' Union – both PKI mass organizations – fought against forced labour (romusha) and encouraged land seizures (aksi sepihak). These campaigns became more and more radical. In February 1965, the Plantation Workers' Union occupied land held by the US Rubber Company in North Sumatra. US Rubber and Goodyear Tires saw this as a direct threat to their interests in Indonesia. Such audacity would not be tolerated. Three multinational oil companies (Caltex, Stanvac and Shell) watched this with alarm. US diplomat George Ball wrote to US National Security Advisor McGeorge Bundy that in 'the long run' events in Indonesia such as these land seizures 'may be more important than South Vietnam'. Ball would know. He oversaw the 1963 coup in South Vietnam against the US ally Ngô Đình Diệm. The West felt it could not stand by as the PKI got more aggressive.

By 1965, the PKI had three million party members – adding a million members in the year. It had emerged as a serious political force in Indonesia, despite the anti-communist military's attempts to squelch its growth. Membership in its mass organizations went up to 18 million. A strange incident – the killing of three generals in Jakarta – set off a massive campaign, helped along by the CIA and Australian intelligence, to excise the communists from Indonesia. Mass murder was the order of the day. The worst killings were in East Java and in Bali. Colonel Sarwo Edhie's forces, for instance, trained militia squads to kill communists. 'We gave them two or three days' training,' Sarwo Edhie told journalist John Hughes, 'then sent them out to kill the communists.' In East Java, one eyewitness recounted, the prisoners were forced to dig a grave, then 'one by one, they were beaten with bamboo clubs, their throats slit, and they were pushed into the mass grave'. By the end of the massacre, a million Indonesian men and women of the left were sent to these graves. Many millions more were isolated, without work and friends. Aidit was arrested by Colonel Yasir Hadibroto, brought to Boyolali (in Central Java) and executed. He was 42.

There was no way for the world communist movement to protect their Indonesian comrades. The USSR's reaction was tepid. The Chinese called it a 'heinous and diabolical' crime. But neither the USSR nor China could do anything. The United Nations stayed silent. The PKI had decided to take a path that was without the guns. Its cadre could not defend themselves. They were not able to fight the military and the anti-communist gangs. It was a bloodbath.

In 1966, national liberation movements came to Havana, Cuba, to inaugurate the Tricontinental. This was to be a platform for those movements that did not put down the gun. Theirs was a reaction to the brutality of the colonial refusal to accept history's verdict and it was a reaction to the massacre in Indonesia. Che Guevara had already left Cuba for the Congo, where he hoped to focus the rebellions across the African continent. He sent a letter to the Tricontinental that was read by Fidel Castro. In his letter, he noted that armed action against imperialism stretched from Vietnam at one end to Venezuela at the other. In the midst of this, Che wrote is 'Indonesia, where we can not assume that the last word has been said, regardless of the annihilation of the Communist Party in that country when the reactionaries took over'.

There was little mention in Havana of the Soviet Union. It had slowed down its support for national liberation movements, eager for detente and conciliation with the West by the mid-1960s. In 1963, Aidit had chastised the Soviets, saying, 'Socialist states are not genuine if they fail to really give assistance to the national liberation struggle'. The reason why parties such as the PKI held fast to 'Stalin' was not because they defended the purges or collectivization in the USSR. It was because 'Stalin' in the debate around militancy had come to stand in for revolutionary idealism and for the anti-fascist struggle. Aidit had agreed that the Soviets could have any interpretation of Stalin in terms of domestic policy ('criticize him, remove his remains from the mausoleum, rename Stalingrad'), but other Communist Parties had the right to assess his role on the international level. He was a 'lighthouse', Aidit said in 1961, whose work was 'still useful to Eastern countries'. This was a statement against the conciliation towards imperialism of the Khrushchev era. It was a position shared across many of the Communist Parties of the Third World.

Many Communist parties, frustrated with the pace of change and with the brutality of the attacks on them, would take to the gun in this period – from Peru to the Philippines. The massacre in Indonesia hung heavily on the world communist movement. But this move to the gun had its limitations, for many of these parties would mistake the tactics of armed revolution for a strategy of violence. The violence worked most effectively the other way. The communists were massacred in Indonesia – as we have seen – and they were butchered in Iraq and Sudan, in Central Asia and South America. The image of communists being thrown from helicopters off the coast of Chile is far less known than any cliché about the USSR.

My volumes of Capital *from 1981.*

Memories of Communism

In 1977, when I was ten, the Left Front won the elections in my native West Bengal. Red flags filled Kolkata, the city where I lived, and demonstrations and processions became an everyday reality. Jyoti Basu, the leader of the CPI (M), became the Chief Minister. He took to the radio on June 22 and offered this as his vision for the state,

> The common people of our state face grave problems in meeting the basic needs of life. Problems have accumulated over the years in all spheres – food, clothing, housing, transport, power, education, health and even with regard to drinking water facilities. The economy of the state is in a moribund condition and the people's suffering knows no bounds. Massive unemployment, closed factories, retrenchments, absence of investment, power shortage – all these problems have assumed frightful proportions. The condition of the countryside beggars description. We shall make serious and sincere efforts to tackle these problems.

He said that the police would not stand on the side of the capitalists and nor would the state bureaucracy work against the popular movements. The Left Front government would go immediately towards land reforms and for the registration of landless rural workers. These immensely popular measures earned the Left popularity in the state and outside it.

Four years later, in 1981, I bought my first edition of Marx's *Capital* – the Progress Publishers edition – which sits now in my mother's flat in Kolkata. I read it slowly, trying to find my way through the complexity of Marx's prose. My aunt had been in the communist movement already. I admired her from afar for her commitment and her stance. I read *Capital* line by line as I read John Reed's *Ten Days that Shook the World* and Marx's writings on the Paris Commune. These books, alongside what was happening in the countryside of West Bengal, were my windows into the world of Communism and to the USSR. I would later find myself at protests and demonstrations, gradually entering the world of the CPI (M) and its mass organizations. My new comrades and I would discuss Indian politics mainly, but also – on occasion – the developments in the world communist movement. Our world into the USSR did not start with 1917, but with our own experiences. We looked at Moscow as a distant cousin, not as a parent.

One of the books that I was able to find at a used bookstore was Leon Trotsky's magisterial *History of the Russian Revolution*. I read this over my puja holidays in 1982, sitting in the Kolkata heat, with a petromax lantern to compensate for the 'load-shedding'. My old copy is marked up – each page with a note. Right at the end, there is a sentence that appealed to me, and still does. It is about how the USSR was never given a chance by the bourgeoisie – as one would expect. From its first days, it was criticized mercilessly. Trotsky wrote his book in 1930, sitting in Istanbul, in exile in Turkey from the USSR. Thirteen years had elapsed since the October Revolution. The revolution was already being derided. 'Capitalism', Trotsky wrote in his conclusion, 'required a hundred years to elevate science and technique to the heights and plunge humanity into the hell of war and crisis. To socialism its enemies allow only fifteen years to create and furnish a terrestrial paradise. We took no such obligation upon ourselves. We never set these dates. The process of vast transformation must be measured by an adequate scale.' But it did not have the time to develop.

The USSR lasted only seventy years. This is a very small period of time in the scope of world history. Its achievements have been pilloried – its demise being the greatest argument against its achievements. But merely because it disappeared does not mean that it was without merit. It provides us with the assurance that a workers' and peasants' state can exist, that it can create policies to benefit the vast masses of the people rather than merely the rich, that it can heal and educate rather than simply starve and kill. This is something to hold on to.

'By creating a new, Soviet type of State,' Lenin wrote in 1918, 'we solved only a small part of this difficult problem. The principal difficulty lies in the economic sphere'. To socialize production was not going to be easy. An attack by the forces opposed to the October Revolution – including most Western powers – threw the new government into disarray. The Red Army had to be organized to defend the new state, which meant resources began to be drained away from social uses. At no point during its seven decades, did the Soviet Union exist without major external threats. Its entire architecture of socialist planning was constrained by the imperatives of security.

The USSR chose to push for rapid economic growth to sustain the Red Army and to provide sufficient social wealth to improve the livelihood of the population. There was consistently a worry that the use of strategies to build industrial capacity in a hurry and to increase rural productivity would lead to far too centralized a state. 'Communists have become bureaucrats', warned Lenin in 1918 in a letter to Grigori Sokolnikov, one of his closest comrades. 'If anything will destroy us, it is this'. Embattled by the siege, driven by the hurry to build the physical plant and the human capacity of the country, pushed by classes adverse to their experiments, the Soviets moved to weaken democratic institutions. Their choices were few. It is in this lack of choices that some of the major institutional errors crept in for the Soviet Union.

The small Bolshevik Party renamed the Communist Party of the Soviet Union drew in three million members by 1933. It was a dynamic party, which enthused popular classes into new activity – including exciting new developments in culture, art, philosophy, technical sciences, and so on. The great advances in the imagination seemed to come from nowhere, but, actually, they came from the spirit of the revolution and from its instrument, the Party. When the Party began to go against the opposition, it excised the potential richness of Soviet politics and left the Party in a weakened position. Party members became *apparatchiks* in the bureaucracy, denuding the political life of the party for the administrative life of the state. With the Tsar's apparatus in their European exile, it was necessary to staff the bureaucracy with every capable person. Party members had to be dragooned from their role as organizers of the working class and the peasantry into bureaucrats. This partly emptied the Party of its life. It did not help that so many vibrant Party members – Sokolnikov among them, but so too the linguist Voloshinov, the literary scholar Medvedev, the theatre director Meyerhold, the botanist Vavilov, the pianist Gayibova – were killed in the Purges. The Party suffered greatly from the loss of these talented people either to State jobs or to the gallows.

The advances, despite the setbacks, were quite incredible. Planning as a mechanism drew the admiration of capitalist state managers. It allowed the USSR to better apportion the meagre resources toward rapid industrial growth. The physical plant is precisely what built the bulwark of the USSR against fascism. There is no question that Western liberalism was saved by the might of the USSR in World War II. If the USSR had not broken through as a result of War Communism, the New Economic Policy, and Stalin's industrialization policy, then Western Europe would have been broken by decades of fascism. As it happened, Hitler's ambitions died in the factory towns of the USSR, where the steel and mortar emerged to destroy the Wehrmacht. World War II devastated the USSR, which had to go onto a War Communism footing to build up its strength. The Western encirclement had begun again as it had right after 1917. There was no respite for the Soviet Union, which had lost over twenty-six million people in the defence of freedom. Not enough can be said of the great sacrifices of the Soviet people in general. Tragically, the fruit of their sacrifice was seized by liberalism and not by Communism.

One of the major limitations of the USSR was that it did not enhance the democratic aspirations of the people. In fact, by restriction of democracy, it allowed the West – only formally democratic – to claim the mantle of democracy. Friedrich Engels wrote of the February 1848 uprising, 'Our age, the age of democracy, is breaking'. He described the scene in the French Chamber of Deputies when a worker rushed in with a pistol in hand. 'No more deputies', he shouted, 'We are the masters.' It was not to be in 1848. But this is the seam in communism that is irrepressible – the desire for participation and leadership. In October 1917, Lenin addressed this possibility directly. 'We are not utopians', he wrote. 'We know that an unskilled labourer or a cook cannot immediately get on with a job of state administration.' The key word here is 'immediately'. Training is essential, Lenin wrote, and once trained, every cook can govern. 'Our revolution will be invincible', he continued, 'if it is not afraid of itself, if it transfers all power to the proletariat.' That transfer of power did not effectively happen – although the Supreme Soviet was much more representative of the working class and peasantry than any liberal democracy, and its leadership came from solid working-class (Brezhnev) and peasant (Khrushchev) backgrounds. The full promise of Communism could not, however, be met in the constraints of the USSR.

The lack of effective democracy meant that there became a tendency to bureaucracy and to stagnation – bolstered by the diversion of an enormous amount of the social surplus to the security establishment. Attempts at reform of the system – such as Kosygin's 1965, 1973 and 1979 reforms – would be ill-starred. These were top-down initiatives. They did not emerge from the depths of the party and of the population. It was a similar top-down attempt in the 1980s led by Gorbachev that led to the liquidation of the USSR. Gorbachev went for openness (*Glasnost*) and economic restructuring (*perestroika*), introducing these Russian words into English. Similar policies had been pushed in China around this time, and much of what he had attempted was in the framework of Kosygin's various attempts at reform. What Gorbachev did most dramatically was to insist on multiparty elections and to essentially frontally attack the role of the Communist Party in the USSR. There was a word for this – *demokratizatsiya* – the dismantling of the state institutions, which were then left prey to the opportunistic party *apparatchiks* and private businessmen who became the first Russian oligarchs – those men fed on the social wealth produced by the Soviet people. The precipitous break-up of the state allowed unscrupulous politicians such as Boris Yeltsin (along with his intellectual cronies Anatoly Chubais and Yegor Gaidar) to drive the USSR off the cliff. In fact, what is often not raised in this connection is that Yeltsin, with the support of General Pavel Grachev, conducted a *coup d'état* against the USSR in October 1993. This was the October Counter-Revolution.

The Soviet Union collapsed in 1991. The great social wealth was then turned over to an oligarchy. The social deterioration was rapid. The British medical journal, *The Lancet*, estimated that over a million Russians died 'due to the economic shock of mass privatization and shock therapy' in the decade from 1991 to 2001. Life expectancy for the Russian male was 65 in the last days of the USSR, but it collapsed to 60 a decade later. Inequality and sorrow returned to the new republics that emerged out of the USSR. No wonder then that polls routinely find that more than half of the Russian citizens dream of a return to the days of the USSR.

All of this was clear to us in the CPI (M) and in other Third World Communist movements. Amílcar Cabral had already warned from the stage of the Tricontinental in 1966, 'We must practice revolutionary democracy in every aspect of our Party life. Hide nothing from the masses of our people. Tell no lies. Expose lies whenever they are told. Mask no difficulties, mistakes, failures. Claim no easy victories. . . .' In 1990, the CPI (M)'s

Central Committee warned that developments in the USSR would soon catapult into its destruction. 'The concept of proletarian dictatorship was reduced to the dictatorship of the party and this at times to the dictatorship of the leading coterie of the party'. Democracy within the USSR had suffered. The working class and peasantry had lost their hold on the country. It was going to be delivered to a new class that would not pursue a socialist path. When the USSR collapsed, we – in the orbit of the CPI (M) – were not surprised, even as we mourned its loss for the Soviet people and for world politics.

The USSR's fall came at the same time as India surrendered to the International Monetary Fund and as India's social and political world was convulsed by political violence along religious lines. On December 6, 1992, fascistic forces in India destroyed a 16th-century mosque. In West Bengal, the Left Front gave a call for people to create a 700-kilometre human chain from the Bay of Bengal to the mountains of the Himalayas. I remember standing at the Hazra crossing in Kolkata, holding hands with other comrades in a line that seemed to stretch outwards to infinity in both directions. There was an electric feeling here of being part of a movement that was against fascism and against capitalism, that was for human freedom at its highest. We were strangers, most of us, but we were linked together to make not just 'another world', but a socialist world, a world of fellowship and care, of values that had propelled the Bolsheviks to their revolution in 1917. It is a feeling that I carry with me now.

The fall of the USSR hit Cuba very hard, since its economy had come to rely upon trade with the Eastern bloc. The Cuban leadership watched with alarm as the USSR removed its troops from the island and as the USSR backed off from its commitments in Nicaragua and Angola. It seemed that the new government in the USSR – led by Gorbachev – was rolling back Soviet power in anticipation of a surrender to the West. This is precisely how Castro articulated it in 1991. In an interview with the Mexican journal

Siempre, Castro offered his assessment of what was happening to the USSR – seventy years after the revolution. It is worthwhile to read the entire answer he gave when asked if the dissolution of the USSR was inevitable,

> I do not think that those changes were historically inevitable. I cannot think that way. I cannot adopt that fatalistic approach, because I do not think that the return to capitalism and the disappearance of the socialist field was inevitable. I think that subjective factors played an important role in this process. There were all kinds of mistakes, for example, the divorce from the masses. If we were to delve deeply into this subject, we would say that there were large ideological weaknesses because the masses moved away from the ideals of socialism, among which human solidarity is primary. The real values of socialism were being neglected, and the material questions received more attention as time went by. The ideological part of this kind of process was being neglected, while the materialistic part was being stressed. It suddenly appeared as if the objective of socialism, according to the statements, speeches, and documents, had focused only on improving the standard of living of the population every year: A little more cloth fabric, a little more cheese, a little more milk, a little more ham, more material stuff. To me, socialism is a total change in the life of the people and the establishment of new values and a new culture which should be based mainly on solidarity between people, not selfishness and individualism.

Socialism is a total change in the life of the people: this is the most important point made not only by Castro but by the Cuban revolutionary experience. It is something that I believe is the most important lesson from the history of socialist experimentation thus far. The USSR will be remembered for its breakthrough against monarchy, its emancipation of the peasantry and the working class, its war against fascism and its support for the anti-colonial movements; it cannot be reduced entirely to the purges or the failure to produce a wide range of commodities. But it should also be remembered for having failed to deepen our understanding of socialist democracy and of a socialist culture. These are the challenges before us. We have to develop new ideas to deepen the meaning of socialism, a living tradition not a dead past.

Today, in many parts of the world, despite the collapse of the USSR, the red flag remains aloft in our movements. Who carries this red flag? Brave women and men who believe in a cause that is greater than their own self-interest, who believe that whatever the errors made over the course of the past century, the dream of socialism remains alive and well. These brave women and men look up at the sky and see the red star over their world.